KID TRAILBLAZERS

TRUE TALES OF CHILDHOOD FROM

INFLUENCERS AND LEADERS

STORIES BY *ROBIN STEVENSON*   ILLUSTRATIONS BY *ALLISON STEINFELD*

KAMALA HARRIS STACEY ABRAMS AI WEIWEI GRETA THUNBERG

KID TRAILBLAZERS

TRUE TALES OF CHILDHOOD FROM

INFLUENCERS AND LEADERS

STORIES BY *ROBIN STEVENSON* ILLUSTRATIONS BY *ALLISON STEINFELD*

ELLIOT PAGE SHONDA RHIMES JOHN LEWIS BENAZIR BHUTTO

Library of Congress Cataloging-in-Publication Data
Names: Stevenson, Robin, 1968- author. | Steinfeld, Allison, illustrator.
Title: Kid trailblazers : true tales of childhood from influencers and leaders /
stories by Robin Stevenson ; illustrations by Allison Steinfeld.
Other titles: True tales of childhood from influencers and leaders
Description: Philadelphia, PA : Quirk Books, [2022] | Series: Kid legends
Includes bibliographical references and index. | Audience: Ages 9-12
Summary: "Childhood biographies of sixteen changemakers in government,
social activism, environmental justice, and the arts"—Provided by publisher.
Identifiers: LCCN 2021057242 (print) | LCCN 2021057243 (ebook)
ISBN 9781683693017 (hardcover) | ISBN 9781683693130 (ebook)
Subjects: LCSH: Biography—Juvenile literature. | Children—Biography—
Juvenile literature. | Politicians—Biography—Juvenile literature.
Political activists—Biography—Juvenile literature.
Artists—Biography—Juvenile literature.
Classification: LCC CT107 .S774 2022 (print) | LCC CT107 (ebook)
DDC 920.02—dc23/eng/20211214
LC record available at https://lccn.loc.gov/2021057242
LC ebook record available at https://lccn.loc.gov/2021057243

ISBN: 978-1-68369-301-7

Printed in Singapore

Typeset in Bulmer MT, Bell MT, Linowrite, and Bulldog

Designed by Andie Reid and Ryan Hayes
Illustrations by Allison Steinfeld
Production management by John J. McGurk

Quirk Books
215 Church Street
Philadelphia, PA 19106
quirkbooks.com

10 9 8 7 6 5 4 3 2 1

To Patience Batamuliza,
with so much love and respect

Table of Contents

PART 3

Protecting Our Planet

PART 4

Harnessing the Power of Art

Introduction

Do you ever look around and see things you want to change? Are you the kind of person who likes to take the lead? Do you dream of a world where people are truly free and equal, where our planet is protected, and where everyone's voice can be heard?

Maybe you will be a trailblazer! Our world is always evolving, and many changes are driven by people like you: people who want to make a difference and are willing to lead the way and blaze new trails.

Some trailblazers are politicians, working to help our governments do a better job of representing all the people they serve. Others are activists, leading social movements, fighting for human rights, or taking a stand for environmental justice. And some are artists, writers, actors, filmmakers, or poets. They use their art and their words to challenge established ideas, to make people think, and to raise awareness of issues they are passionate about.

Trailblazers organize protests, hold meetings, run for office, raise money, and go on strike. They influence people through social media, write books, and create television shows. They send letters, take photographs, share their poems, and demonstrate in the streets. There are many ways to lead the way, influence people, and make change!

Throughout history, courageous people have stepped up to tackle big problems, and our world today is a better place because of their efforts. There is still lots of work to do, but luckily there are also lots of great role models to learn from. Today's trailblazers stand on the shoulders of those who came before them and are leading the way for those who come after them. And whether they are government leaders, activists, or artists, they all have one thing in common: they started out as kids.

Before she wrote television shows, Shonda Rhimes acted out stories with cans of vegetables in her mom's pantry. And civil rights activist and US congressman John Lewis was once a little boy who preached sermons to his family's chickens.

But for many of the trailblazers in this book, childhood was not a carefree time. Some lacked even the most basic of freedoms.

Scientist and environmental activist David Suzuki spent his childhood in an internment camp, imprisoned by the Canadian government along with thousands of other Japanese Canadians. The Chinese artist Ai Weiwei grew up in exile, living in an underground dugout at the edge of China's Gobi Desert.

Being a trailblazer takes confidence; you have to be able to stand up for yourself in the face of opposition. So it helps to have people who believe in you. Stacey Abrams's father always told her to fight for what she wanted. Kamala Harris had a mother who raised her to believe she could grow up to do anything.

And of course, you don't have to wait until you are grown up to make change! Greta Thunberg was just fifteen when she started her school strike for the climate.

At twelve years old, Marley Dias began her campaign to collect and donate a thousand books about Black girls. And Mari Copeny was only eight when she made national headlines in the United States by writing to President Barack Obama about the lack of safe water in her community.

Without the trailblazers in this book, our world would be a very different place. Their paths weren't always easy, but they persevered, overcoming all kinds of obstacles to achieve their goals. I hope their stories will inspire you to follow your own dreams and stand up for what you believe . . . and to change the world for the better!

ONE

STANDING UP FOR DEMOCRACY

LEADING

GOVERNMENTS

★ ★ AND ★ ★

WORKING

FOR CHANGE,

— THESE —

KID TRAILBLAZERS

— BROKE BARRIERS AND INSPIRED —

YOUNG FUTURE

LEADERS

from around

THE WORLD.

Benazir Bhutto

My Place

When Benazir Bhutto was elected prime minister of Pakistan, she became the first woman to lead a Muslim country. As a little kid, she loved hearing her father tell stories about the country's history and their family's place in it.

Benazir's father, **Zulfikar Ali Bhutto,** was born in Larkana, in southeastern Pakistan. His family home, known as Al-Murtaza, was a huge house surrounded by beautiful gardens. Benazir's grandfather, Sir Shah Nawaz, built Al-Murtaza. He valued education and sent all his children to school. Zulfikar studied in both California and England before returning to Pakistan to be a lawyer.

Benazir's mother, Nusrat Ispahani, was from a wealthy Iranian Kurdish family and had attended university in Iran before emigrating to Pakistan. Nusrat and Zulfikar met in the city of Karachi and were married in 1951. Benazir was born two years later on June 21, 1953. As a baby, she had very rosy cheeks, which led to her nickname: Pinkie. A year later, her brother Murtaza was born, followed by her sister, Sanam, and her youngest brother, Shah Nawaz.

The Bhutto family had lived in Pakistan's Sindh province for hundreds of years. Benazir's ancestors owned much of the land in the area, and several villages are named for them. Their home at Al-Murtaza was near the ancient ruins of an Indus civilization from 2500 BC. The ruins were called Moenjadaro, but when Benazir was young, she thought the name was Munj Jo Dero—which means "my place" in Sindhi. She was proud to come from a place with so much history and loved hearing her father's stories about it.

When Benazir was four years old, her father began working at the United Nations. For seven years, she rarely saw him—except when she spotted his picture in the newspaper! She read about her father negotiating agreements with other countries or speaking up for Pakistan at the United Nations. Benazir's mother usually traveled with her husband, so Benazir was often left at home with the household staff and her siblings. "Look after the other children," her parents would remind her. "You are the oldest."

Benazir's mother gave her money for food and household supplies, which she hid under her pillow. At night, she climbed onto a kitchen stool and pretended to review her financial accounts. At the time, just two dollars would buy food for the whole household!

When she was five, Benazir started school at the Convent of Jesus and Mary. Although it was a Catholic school, some wealthy Muslim families sent their children there because it was considered one of the best schools in the city. At home, she spoke her parents' languages, Sindhi and Persian, or Pakistan's national language, Urdu. At school, she was taught in English. After school, she and her brothers studied the Quran. "We spent hours struggling over the difficult Arabic," Benazir recalled. When she was nine, she began praying with her mother, who taught Benazir the traditions and rituals of prayer. Her mother took her religious faith seriously, never failing to pray five times a day, even when she was busy or traveling.

The prophet Muhammad had called for the education of women and supported women's rights, Benazir's parents told her. They taught her that Muslim history was filled with women who had done important public deeds—and they were determined that she would be the first girl in the family to study abroad. "You will all pack your suitcases and I will take you to the airport to see you off," her father used to tell his children. "Pinkie will leave as a scruffy little kid and come back a beautiful young lady in a sari."

Benazir's father encouraged her to take an interest in politics and history, and he talked to Benazir about events that were happening in the world around her. When she was ten years old, he shook her awake in the middle of the night. "This is no time to sleep," he told her, and explained that the president of the United States, John F. Kennedy—a man he had met and admired—had been shot.

That same year, she and her little sister, Sanam, were sent away to boarding school in Murree. Her father wanted to make sure they didn't get special treatment because of his wealth or his status, so he told the nuns to treat his daughters exactly like the other kids. "For the first time I had to make my own bed, polish my shoes, carry water for bathing and toothbrushing back and forth from the water taps in the corridors," Benazir recalled.

While she was away at school, Benazir's father wrote her a long letter about what was happening at the United Nations. He described how the world's most powerful countries were primarily interested in their own affairs, neglecting developing countries like Pakistan. One of the nuns read the letter aloud to her and Sanam, but it was much too complicated for them to understand. They were not yet interested in world events and preferred playing jacks with goat bones or reading British novels by Enid Blyton.

Then, in 1965, something happened that brought political affairs crashing into their school life: India and Pakistan went to war over Kashmir. People in Pakistan were afraid India might invade. The school held air raid drills, during which older girls were responsible for getting younger ones into a bomb shelter. Benazir made her sister tie her slippers to her feet at bedtime, so that in the event of a drill Sanam wouldn't have to waste time looking for them. Many of the students had fathers who were army officers or important government officials, and Benazir recalled, "we gave each other false names and practiced them in case we fell into the hands of our enemies . . . we were all quite dramatic about the possibility of being kidnapped." The war lasted for only two and half weeks, but it was a frightening time.

When Benazir was fourteen, her father formed a new political party: the Pakistan People's Party. The PPP promoted democratic ideas and promised more help for people living in poverty. The Bhutto family home in Karachi doubled as the party's office. Every day, people lined up at their gates to join the party. Benazir and Sanam paid the small fee to become official party members and helped sign up others.

The country had been under military rule for many years, and many people who were in powerful positions were not happy about a new political party forming.

Benazir's father began receiving threats. "I tried not to show my fear," Benazir recalled. "I didn't even allow myself to feel frightened." Less than a year after forming the new party, while Benazir was taking exams and applying to university, her father was arrested and jailed.

There were protests and riots in Karachi, so Benazir's mother told her to stay at home. Benazir coped with her worries by throwing herself into her studies and by distracting herself with swimming and squash games at the nearby sports club. Her father wrote to her from prison, telling her how proud he was of her accomplishments. "At this rate, you might become the president," he wrote—and recommended a long list of books she should read to further educate herself.

Three months later, Benazir's father was released from jail. Soon after that, she learned that she had been accepted to study at Radcliffe College in the United States. Because she was only sixteen, she had to get special permission to begin university early. Moving halfway across the world was a difficult adjustment, but Benazir later called those university years the happiest of her life.

Back at home in Pakistan, her father became the country's first democratically elected prime minister. Her mother was ill, and so Benazir accompanied her father to important political events and met leaders from many countries. Her father wanted her to study in England just like he had, so after graduating from Radcliffe she went to Oxford, where she became president of the university's debating society. After she graduated in 1977, she returned to Pakistan. That same year, the military took back control of the country and Benazir's father was executed.

Heartbroken but determined, Benazir and her mother took control of the PPP and led a movement to restore democracy in the country. They were imprisoned and then exiled to Britain, but Benazir never gave up on her country. She returned to Pakistan, and in 1988, she led the party to victory, becoming the first woman prime minister in a Muslim country. Only thirty-five years old, she was also one of the youngest women to ever become a government leader. Sadly, she was assassinated in December 2007, after giving a speech at a political rally in the city of Rawalpindi.

Benazir faced many challenges during her time in politics, and she was sometimes a controversial figure, but she always worked hard to give hope to the people of her country. She became a symbol for women's rights around the world, and she inspired many Pakistani girls and women—including the young activist Malala Yousafzai, who hung a poster of Benazir on her wall at university.

Angela Merkel

Behind
the
Iron
Curtain

As the first woman chancellor of Germany, Angela Merkel led her country from 2005 to 2021. She has had an extraordinary influence in Europe, advocating for freedom, democracy, equality, and human rights—but she grew up in a Communist dictatorship where freedom was more a dream than a reality.

Nearly ten years before Angela's birth, at the end of the Second World War, Germany was split into two separate countries. West Germany was a democratic country controlled by the Allies, and East Germany— or the German Democratic Republic (GDR)—was a Communist country controlled by the Soviet Union. The capital city of Berlin was divided into two zones, but people could move freely between them. The political boundary between Western countries and the Soviet Union and its dependent allies in Central Europe was known as the Iron Curtain.

Angela Dorothea Kasner was born on July 17, 1954, in the West German city of Hamburg—the city that hamburgers take their name from! Her father, Horst Kasner, was a Lutheran pastor, and her mother,

Herlind Jentzsch, was an English and Latin teacher. Angela was their first child.

At the time Angela was born, many thousands of people were fleeing Soviet-controlled East Germany. For both political and economic reasons, they wanted to live in the West. When Angela was just three months old, her family did something very unusual: they travelled in the opposite direction. They moved first to the East German village of Quitzow and then, when Angela was three years old, to the small country town of Templin, about fifty miles north of Berlin. It was a beautiful place with lakes and rivers, canals and old buildings, and many farms. Angela's father had been asked to run the local Lutheran church and to set up a seminary to teach new clergy.

The Kasner family lived at a large estate known as the Waldhof, which means "forest court" in German. The Waldhof was part of a complex run by the church to house and employ people with developmental disabilities. It was a very safe and pleasant environment for a child to grow up in. Angela's family lived on the top floor of a house that they shared with students. The family had goats and chickens and a small vegetable garden, and the gardener became young Angela's good friend. Soon, two younger siblings came along: Marcus, who was three years younger than Angela, and Irene, who was ten years younger. Angela, who went by the nickname Kasi, short for Kasner, said she was a very clumsy kid who could barely walk downhill without falling.

Angela's paternal grandparents lived in West Berlin. Her grandfather died when she was only five, but Angela often visited her grandmother Margarethe and spent part of her holidays with her each summer. Margarethe encouraged Angela to take an interest in art and music. "Those were wonderful times, complete childhood happiness. I was allowed to watch television until ten in the evening," Angela recalled. While staying in Berlin, she "systematically visited all the museums one by one."

But when Angela was seven, everything changed. Her family was on their way home from vacationing in Bavaria when Angela's father noticed something strange. There were a surprising number of soldiers around, and he saw a lot of barbed wire being stored in the woods. He felt uneasy—but no one could have predicted what was about to happen. Three days later, on August 13, 1961, the final part of the border between East Germany and West Germany was closed. Overnight, East German troops erected fences along the border, and soon these fences were replaced with concrete blocks. In the city of Berlin, a wall was being built. Travelling between the two countries was no longer possible.

On both sides of the wall, people were shocked and horrified. Angela's father preached a sermon, prayers were said in church, and her mother sobbed all day. Angela and her parents, like everyone on the eastern side of the wall, were suddenly locked in and unable to leave. They were separated from their relatives, their family was divided, and they had lost their freedom. It would be another fifteen years before Angela would travel to any Western country.

She later said that the day the Berlin Wall went up was her first political memory. Her family never accepted the divided Germany, and political discussions and debates were common around the dinner table. They secretly watched the news on television, and Angela knew the names of all the West German politicians. When she was fourteen, she hid in the school restroom, listening to the election of a new West German president on her transistor radio. Her relatives in West Germany sent care packages of items that weren't available in East Germany—including jeans for Angela!

In East Germany, it wasn't safe to openly discuss your political views. Angela learned to be careful, and to keep her opinions to herself. "Learning when to keep quiet was a great advantage in the GDR period," she later said. "It was one of our survival strategies."

The year the Berlin Wall went up was the same year that Angela started school. One of her former classmates later said, "She was very quiet . . . but very nice and friendly, and extraordinarily intelligent." Her math teacher remembered her as a very gifted student, someone who never gave up on a tough problem.

She also had a talent for languages. She practiced English by reading a Communist newspaper from the UK, called the *Morning Star*. At school, she excelled in Russian, and she took advantage of the opportunity to practice speaking it when soldiers from the Soviet military base came into town. She competed in a national Russian-language competition with students two years older than her—and came in third place! The prize? A trip to Moscow, where she bought an album by the Beatles. Two years later, in grade ten, Angela competed again. This time, she won.

Angela's parents encouraged her to work hard and to fit in. As a teenager, she became a member of the Free German Youth—the Communist youth organization sponsored by the government. Joining these groups was technically voluntary—but those who

didn't join might find themselves unable to get into university. Besides, her parents pointed out, the group might help her develop her leadership skills. Angela won a medal and was commended for her "outstanding socialist engagement."

In 1968, when Angela was fourteen, she and her family visited Czechoslovakia. There, people were beginning to talk about democracy, wanting change and greater freedom to travel and express their views. It was an exciting and hopeful time known as the Prague Spring—but that August, the Soviet army invaded the country and crushed the democratic movement.

This trip had a powerful impact on Angela's political views, and it left her with a passion for travel. Curious about the world outside East Germany and always ready for a new adventure, Angela was eager to explore. While still in high school, she began travelling with friends. They were not free to visit the West, but they backpacked around Central Europe, visiting resorts on the Black Sea and exploring cities like Prague, Bucharest, and Budapest—the last of which, Angela imagined, must be a bit like London.

During her last year of high school, she and some friends found themselves in trouble after they put on a performance at their school's cultural festival fundraiser. They were expected to raise money for a Vietnamese resistance group fighting against the United States, but instead they collected money for a freedom movement in Mozambique. They performed a cheeky poem—and then finished by singing in English, which was considered the language of the enemy. In the tightly controlled dictatorship, this kind of teenage rebelliousness was dangerous. Angela's university studies were at risk. Luckily for her, her father was able to use his position within the church to get her out of trouble, and after she graduated from high school, Angela attended Karl Marx University in Leipzig. She decided to study physics—she had done poorly in physics during high school and was determined to prove she could conquer the subject.

Some people tried to escape East Germany, digging tunnels under the Berlin Wall or parachuting over it, but Angela just got on with her life. At university, she met a physics student named Ulrich Merkel, whom she eventually married. She later said, "I decided that if the system became too terrible, I would have to try to escape. But if it wasn't too bad, then I wouldn't lead my life in opposition to the system, because I was scared of the damage that would do to me." But although Angela didn't want to challenge the Communist Party, she didn't want to join it either. When she applied for a job and was told by officials that she would be expected to become an informant and spy on her colleagues, she told them that she'd make a very bad spy because she was terrible at keeping secrets! It worked; they left her alone.

After graduating in 1986 with a doctorate degree in quantum chemistry, Angela worked briefly as a research scientist. But then, in 1990, the Berlin Wall came down. East and West Berlin were once again a single city—and the capital of a united Germany. New freedoms and possibilities opened up for Angela, and within a month, she became involved in the democracy movement.

Angela went on to become chancellor of Germany, breaking barriers as the first woman to hold this position and the first chancellor to be raised in East Germany. She led the country for sixteen years, facing challenges—a global recession, climate change, the refugee crisis, and a pandemic—with a calm, scientific, analytical intelligence and a strong sense of ethics. After growing up in a country where news was censored, travel was forbidden, and speaking your mind was dangerous, Angela chose to use her power to promote freedom and democracy.

When she was elected president in 2016, **Tsai Ing-wen** became the first woman leader of Taiwan. Under her leadership, Taiwan became the first country in Asia to legalize same-sex marriage—and during the COVID-19 pandemic, her government helped create an effective contact tracing program to minimize the spread of illness, making Taiwan's pandemic response a model for other countries. A strong global advocate for freedom and democracy, Tsai Ing-wen is respected in her own country and by many people around the world. In the People's Republic of China, however, she is frequently attacked by the state media; China considers Taiwan to be part of its territory and does not recognize its democratically elected government. Tsai Ing-wen has worked to strengthen Taiwan's international relationships—a very complicated undertaking, but one she has approached with patience and skill.

Kamala Harris

> Capable
> of Anything

I n 2021, Kamala Harris stepped into the role of vice president of the United States. This was groundbreaking: not only was she the first woman vice president, she was also the first Black vice president and the first vice president of South Asian descent!

Kamala was born in Oakland, California, on October 20, 1964. Her father, Donald Harris, was born in Jamaica. He immigrated to the United States to attend the University of California, Berkeley. Kamala's mother, Shyamala Gopalan, was born in India. She also moved to California to study at Berkeley, travelling over 8,000 miles away from her family while she was still a teenager. Both Shyamala and Donald became involved in the American civil rights movement. They met in 1962 and married the following year.

Eventually, Donald became a professor of economics at Stanford, and Shyamala became a breast cancer researcher. They had two daughters: Kamala, whose name comes from the Sanskrit word for lotus flower, and two years later, her younger sister, Maya.

Kamala's early childhood was happy. She loved playing outdoors. "I remember that when I was a little girl, my father wanted me to run free," she wrote. "'Run, Kamala,' he used to say. 'As fast as you can. Run!' I would take off, the wind in my face, with the feeling that I could do anything." Kamala said she has many memories of her mother putting Band-Aids on her scraped knees!

When Kamala was five, her parents separated. Kamala, Maya, and their mother moved into the top floor of a duplex in a Berkeley neighborhood, where they quickly became known as "Shyamala and the girls." Kamala and her sister still saw their dad, but they were raised primarily by their mother. Kamala said, "She was the one responsible for shaping us into the women we would become. . . . She was smart and tough and fierce and protective. She was generous, loyal, and funny." Shyamala had high expectations for her daughters, but she always made them feel special. She raised them to believe they could do anything they wanted as long as they were willing to work for it.

Because Shyamala had no relatives in the United States, her friends became like family to her. "From almost the moment she arrived from India, she chose and was welcomed to and enveloped in the Black community," Kamala explained. Kamala thought of her mother's close friends as her aunts and uncles. One of them was her Uncle Sherman. He was a skilled chess player, and Kamala often played with him. He enjoyed talking with her about strategy, explaining that you needed to think many moves ahead to outsmart your opponent. Occasionally, he let Kamala win.

Shyamala came from a family that valued political activism; Kamala's grandfather was involved in India's struggle to gain independence from Britain, and her grandmother was a community organizer. "She was born with a sense of justice imprinted on her soul," Kamala said.

Kamala grew up seeing her mother and her mother's friends protesting for civil rights and against the Vietnam War. "I have young memories of a sea of legs moving about, of the energy and shouts and chants,"

Kamala recalled. Her mother used to tell a story about a time a very young Kamala was fussing in her stroller during a demonstration. Kamala explained, "She leaned down to ask me, 'Kamala, what's wrong? What do you want?' and I wailed back, 'Fweedom.'"

FWEEDOM!

Shyamala helped her daughters stay connected to their family in India. Sometimes they made the long trip to spend time with their relatives, but between visits, there were phone calls, letters, and cards. Even though she grew up far from India, Kamala had close relationships to her family there and a strong appreciation for Indian culture. She was proud of her South Asian roots.

Every morning, Kamala would drink a cup of Carnation Instant Breakfast and take the bus to school.

When she started kindergarten in 1969, the city of Berkeley was in the second year of its plan to desegregate elementary schools by busing Black, white, Asian American, and Mexican American kids from their neighborhoods to schools where they could all learn together. Thanks to busing, Kamala's school, Thousand Oaks Elementary School, taught a diverse group of students; Kamala learned to count in multiple languages and celebrated the holidays of many cultures. Her first-grade teacher, Mrs. Wilson, was so committed to her students that she even attended Kamala's law school graduation many years later!

Shyamala worked long days at a research lab, so Kamala and Maya spent time at an after-school program run by their neighbors, the Shelton family.

There, Kamala and Maya learned about leaders and activists like Frederick Douglass, Harriet Tubman, Sojourner Truth, and George Washington Carver. Regina Shelton was like "a second mother" to Kamala and her sister, and at the Shelton house there were always lots of kids to play with, and delicious pound cakes and flaky biscuits to devour.

Kamala's mother also liked to cook, and in the evenings, the kitchen smelled wonderful. Shyamala cooked both soul food and Indian food, seasoning meals from her cupboard full of spices, and Kamala loved to watch. Her mother cooked like a scientist, always experimenting. "Even my lunch became a lab for her creations," Kamala said. Her friends ate PB&Js but Kamala never knew what she'd find inside her brown paper lunch bag. Of course, Kamala admitted, "not every experiment was successful." Shyamala baked too. If Kamala or her sister needed cheering up, their mom sometimes surprised them with an unbirthday party— complete with unbirthday cake and unbirthday presents!

One time, Kamala found a recipe for lemon bars in one of her mother's cookbooks. She worked all afternoon, and when the bars were done, they looked perfect. She proudly carried them over to the Sheltons' house. Unfortunately, Kamala had used salt instead of sugar! But instead of spitting out her first bite, Mrs. Shelton managed to keep a straight face as she told Kamala that it was delicious: "maybe just a little too much salt . . . but really delicious!" Kamala felt like she'd done well despite her mistake. She later wrote, "It was little moments like those that helped me build a natural sense of confidence. I believed I was capable of anything."

The place Kamala loved most of all was Rainbow Sign, a Black cultural center where she and her family often spent their evenings. A warm and welcoming place, it had a huge kitchen, and Kamala remembered that "somebody was always cooking up something delicious—smothered chicken, meatballs in gravy, candied yams, corn bread, peach cobbler."

Rainbow Sign offered classes in dance, theater, art, languages, and more. Many important Black leaders and talented artists visited to give lectures or perform.

Rainbow Sign hosted filmmakers and writers, poets and painters, musicians and dancers, teachers and politicians. The famous writer and civil rights activist James Baldwin was a regular guest.

Because Rainbow Sign welcomed and valued children, Kamala and Maya were able to talk with many of the brilliant performers, leaders, and lecturers who visited the center—politicians like Congresswoman Shirley Chisholm and writers like Alice Walker and Maya Angelou. The Bay Area was "bursting with black pride," Kamala recalled. "Kids like me who spent time at Rainbow Sign were exposed to dozens of extraordinary men and women who showed us what we could become."

But when Kamala was twelve, she got some shocking news. The family was moving to the city of

Montreal, in Canada. Shyamala was excited about her new job, but Kamala was horrified. A new school, in a foreign country, where she imagined everything would be covered in twelve feet of snow! To make it worse, Shyamala sent the girls to the local school, which taught classes in French—and the only French Kamala knew was a few words from her ballet class. Despite this, Kamala and her sister managed to make waves: when the students were forbidden from playing soccer on the school's lawn, they held a demonstration to protest! Kamala recalled, "I'm happy to report that our demands were met."

By the time she was a teenager, Kamala was used to her new life in Canada. Still, she never stopped missing California and planned to return to the United States for college. Kamala was interested in pursuing a career as a lawyer—she saw law "as a tool that can help make things fair." She had seen how people looked to the lawyers in her mom's circle of friends, trusting them to know what to do in difficult situations. "I wanted to be the one people called," she said. "I wanted to be the one who could help."

Civil rights lawyers like Thurgood Marshall and Constance Baker Motley were Kamala's heroes. She decided that she, like Thurgood Marshall, would go to Howard University in Washington, DC. After she graduated, she began her career working in the Alameda County district attorney's office. Kamala was elected district attorney of San Francisco in 2003, and seven years later, she became California's attorney general. In 2017, she became the first South Asian American and second Black woman to serve in the United States Senate.

When Kamala made her first speech as a senator in 2017, she spoke up for the rights of immigrants and refugees. Her own parents were immigrants, she explained. It was her mother's choice to come to America and marry her father that made Kamala's life and her sister's life possible: "It made us Americans, like millions of the children of immigrants before and since." As she criticized the Trump administration's anti-immigrant policies, she spoke of her mother, who had died eight years earlier. "I know she's looking down on us today," she said. "And knowing my mother, she's probably saying, 'Kamala, what on earth is going on down there? We have got to stand up for our values!'"

On January 20, 2021, Joe Biden was inaugurated as president, and Kamala Harris made history. Because of the COVID-19 pandemic, the ceremony was designed to be viewed by an online audience—and more than 33 million people tuned in to watch. For countless girls, and especially girls of color, seeing Kamala step into the role of vice president was a powerful moment—one that carried a message of change and of hope. "While I may be the first woman in this office, I will not be the last," Kamala said. "Every little girl watching tonight sees that this is a country of possibilities."

Stacey Abrams

Never Tell Yourself No

Stacey Abrams is a politician, lawyer, and voting rights activist from Georgia. She is the founder of Fair Fight, an organization that works to protect voting rights and fair elections in the United States. Long before she was old enough to cast a ballot, she used to go to the voting booth with her parents.

Stacey Yvonne Abrams was born on December 9, 1973, in Madison, Wisconsin. Her parents, Carolyn and Robert Abrams, were from Mississippi. They were both from big families; Carolyn was one of seven kids, and Robert was one of six. They met while they were still in their teens, working together as lifeguards. The couple moved to Madison so that Carolyn could study to become a librarian, but they soon returned to Mississippi. Stacey grew up there, in the city of Gulfport, along with her older sister, Andrea, and four younger siblings: Leslie, Richard, Walter, and Jeanine.

Robert's parents were an important part of Stacey's life when she was growing up. Her grandmother's name was Wilter Abrams, but everyone called her Bill. She had raised Stacey's dad and his siblings in poverty, during a time when racial discrimination was legal. Bill and her husband had strong views and expressed them freely, and they taught their children to do the same.

Stacey's dad, Robert, was always a storyteller. "Like any good Southern man, his tales begin with truth and quickly turn fuzzy on the details, weaving the kind of color commentary that holds an audience enraptured. . . . For most of my life, I have heard and memorized his tales, tall and otherwise," Stacey explained. When Robert told stories about his days as a high school football player, the other team got bigger and meaner with every retelling. Stacey's mom told stories too, but hers always had a moral or taught a lesson—and unlike Robert, she never exaggerated for the sake of a good tale.

Stacey's parents shared a love of learning, and each of them had been the first in their families to go to college. But neither Carolyn's job as a librarian nor Robert's job as a shipyard worker paid well, so money was always tight. Sometimes the family couldn't afford running water, electricity, or health care.

Robert and Carolyn wanted their children to get a good education. They managed to find a three-bedroom home in a middle-class area—small for a family of eight, but in a location that allowed Stacey to participate in a program for gifted students at a well-funded school. Looking back, Stacey criticized this unfair system, pointing out that all kids should have high-quality education, no matter where they live or how much money their parents make.

The Abrams family followed three rules that they called the "Trinity for Success": go to church, go to school, and take care of one another. Taking care of one another started at home. Stacey's oldest sister, Andrea, used to organize the kids into games and activities. "We were probably the only kids in our community who played Library," Stacey recalled. Their mom was a librarian, after all, and their house was full of books.

Each of the three oldest girls was responsible for one of their younger siblings. Andrea, who was oldest, looked after baby Jeanine. Leslie cared for little Walter, and Stacey was responsible for Richard. When Richard woke in the morning, he tiptoed into the room Stacey shared with her sister Leslie, and woke her up. Still half asleep, she'd take him to the living room and turn on the TV so he could watch cartoons.

But taking care of one another wasn't just about their family—it was about helping out in the community as well. The Abrams kids volunteered at a soup kitchen and performed plays at juvenile detention centers.

Having made sure their kids could go to a good school, the Abramses were strict about attendance. "My parents said you could miss school if you had a doctor's note and a surgical scar," Stacey said. She recalled, "they taught us to learn for the sake of knowledge itself, and they made certain that we understood no one could take knowledge from us." People could steal your possessions or take away your job, they often pointed out, but no one could take away what was inside your mind.

In middle school, Stacey won a city-wide essay contest. Her dad drove her to the school where she was to pick up her prize. "While he waited in the car, I ran inside to receive my ribbon and my $50 reward," Stacey recalled. "But the woman in charge—white and grim-faced when I introduced myself—refused to give me the money." Stacey could not be the author of the winning essay, the woman told the other people in the lobby. Stacey stood up for herself and demanded her prize, but she was shaken. She experienced many racist incidents like this throughout her childhood, and, she explained, "the repeated doubts took root. What if they were correct?" It took many years for Stacey to regain her confidence.

When Stacey was in her early teens, her family moved to Atlanta, Georgia. Carolyn and Robert both attended university there and became United Methodist ministers. Stacey went to Avondale High School in DeKalb County, Georgia. She wrote poetry for her high school journal and was an excellent student—for the most part. "I was horrible at geometry," she admitted. "It was the first time I took a class where I simply did not understand the concepts. It taught me that even when you're good at things, you're not going to be good at everything."

When Stacey visited her grandparents, aunts, and uncles, she would listen, entranced, as they told stories from the '50s and '60s. Back then, a system called segregation kept white people and Black people apart, sending Black children to different schools from white children, and restricting where Black people could sit, shop, use the bathroom, or even drink from a water fountain. Stacey's grandfather recalled being forced to give up his seat on the bus if a white man wanted to sit down.

Stacey's parents also shared stories: they had graduated from segregated high schools, even though they attended high school more than a decade after the law required schools to be desegregated. In fact, even the swimming pool where Stacey's parents met was racially segregated. They told Stacey about going to the movies as teens and having to sit in what was known as the "colored" section. Both had been involved in the civil rights movement, and her father had been beaten and sent to jail for his activism. Stacey learned about lunch counter sit-ins and discrimination within the health care system—but the thing that most fascinated her was the fight for the right to vote.

Stacey's parents never missed an opportunity to vote. "They raised us to believe our voices would be heard if we too attended every election as though our lives depended on casting that ballot," she said. "I remember following my parents into the school and down the hallway to the gymnasium, where the voting booths stood. . . . My parents would sign in at the table and proceed to the booths with my siblings and me in tow, like the chicks in *Make Way for Ducklings*, one of our favorite storybooks." Their commitment to voting made a big impression on Stacey. "I started a voter-registration drive even before I was old enough to vote," she later said.

The family often discussed politics and voting rights at home. The only time Stacey ever got in a fight at school was because of an argument over the 1980 election between President Jimmy Carter and Ronald Regan. She was six years old! (Stacy later said that Carter lost the election—but she won her fight.)

Stacey was still in high school when she got her first job in politics. She was hired as a typist for a man who was running for Congress. She edited his speech as she typed it and did such a good job that he promoted her to speechwriter.

Stacey graduated from high school as the school's first Black valedictorian and went on to attend Spelman College in Atlanta. While she was studying there, she worked in the Atlanta mayor's office. She also got involved in activism, joining a group called Students for African American Empowerment. They wanted solutions for youth poverty and police violence, and they argued that the racist Confederate battle emblem should be removed from Georgia's state flag.

At age nineteen, Stacey was invited to speak as a youth activist at the thirtieth anniversary March on

Washington, an event commemorating the March on Washington for Jobs and Freedom—the historic 1963 civil rights march where Martin Luther King Jr. gave his famous "I Have a Dream" speech. In front of a large crowd in the nation's capital, Stacey urged everyone listening to include America's young people in working towards jobs, justice, and peace.

Stacey went on to complete a master's degree in public policy at the University of Texas, and then headed to Yale to study law. While she was a law student, she managed to find time to write a novel! It became the first of eight romance books that she published under the pen name Selena Montgomery.

After graduating from law school, Stacey worked as a tax attorney, and then, when she was just twenty-nine, she was appointed a deputy city attorney for the city of Atlanta. Four years later, she ran as a Democrat for the Georgia House of Representatives, where she served for more than a decade. Stacey was the first woman to lead either party in the Georgia state legislature and the first Black party leader in the Georgia House of Representatives.

Stacey never forgot her dad's advice: "Let other people tell you no. Never tell yourself no. If there's something you want, fight for it." In 2018, she ran for governor of Georgia, becoming the first Black woman to be nominated by a major political party in a state governor election.

When she lost that race, she founded Fair Fight to protect voting rights. In the lead-up to the 2020 presidential election, her efforts helped register over 800,000 new voters! She also began writing under her own name, penning two nonfiction books which became best sellers—one on leadership and one on voting rights and democracy. "The act of writing is integral to who I am," she said.

In 2021, Stacey was nominated for a Nobel Peace Prize. And she still isn't telling herself no—even when it comes to possibly running for president. As she says, "you cannot have those things you refuse to dream of."

PART
TWO

FIGHTING FOR BLACK LIVES

MARCHES AND SPEECHES, HASHTAGS AND PROTESTS:

THESE

KID TRAILBLAZERS

LED MOVEMENTS FOR CHANGE

AND INFLUENCED

** PEOPLE **

ACROSS AMERICA

TO SPEAK UP FOR

RACIAL JUSTICE.

Dorothy Pitman Hughes

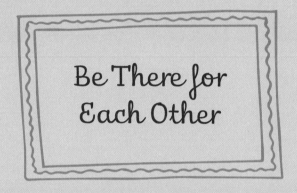

Be There for
Each Other

Dorothy Pitman Hughes is a Black community organizer, feminist, and civil rights activist who travelled all over the United States speaking about race, gender, and class. First, though, she had to find a way out of her tiny community in America's segregated South— by singing!

Dorothy was born in Georgia, in 1938. Her parents were Lessie White and Melton Lee-Ridley, who was usually called Ray. They had eight children; first came Arye Lou and Julia, and then Dorothy, who went by the nickname Dot. Over the next sixteen years, Dorothy became an older sister to Mary, Mildred, Roger, Alice, and Jimmy. The children all called their mother Mudea, short for Mother Dear.

Dorothy grew up in Charles Junction, a timber settlement seven miles north of the small town of Lumpkin, Georgia. It was a close-knit community that included lumber workers and farmers. In fact, all the houses in Charles Junction were rented from a local timber company. "My stubbornness, my will to survive and to make things better—not just for myself but for all the people around me—started in Charles Junction," Dorothy later wrote.

Dorothy's father, Ray, worked as a cook in the US navy during World War II. After the war, he worked as a driver, hauling lumber. Nearly all the other drivers were white, and only Ray had his own truck.

The truck had once been a school bus, but Ray had converted it into a flatbed. Ray drove long distances to deliver lumber. When he came home, he told his children about the places he'd been. For Dorothy, these stories were a window into the wider world, and they sparked her sense of adventure. When she was about twelve, she asked her mom if she could drive the truck. Her mom, who was cooking and not really listening, distractedly said yes—so Dorothy took it out for a spin. Afterwards, she swept over her tire tracks, but her mother wasn't fooled. Still, Dorothy didn't get in trouble . . . After all, she had asked permission!

Ray also held a variety of part time jobs: he was the neighborhood mechanic and wired most of the homes in the community for electricity, and for a while, he worked at a local candy factory. Dorothy and her siblings thought this was great because he often came home with treats for them.

The community they lived in was poor, but Dorothy's family had more money than some. They had chickens and hogs and a big vegetable garden, and they always had enough to eat. One of Dorothy's memories from early childhood involved a white family with two kids who lived across the railroad tracks in a house that had a pecan tree in its yard. Knowing that the food was better at Dorothy's house, the neighbor children would hang around until Dorothy's mom, Lessie, offered to feed them alongside her own kids. "If you were in someone's home at mealtime, you ate there," Dorothy recalled. One Christmas, when Dorothy was nine years old, her siblings and the two neighbor kids had played together all day long. When it was time for Christmas dinner, Lessie asked the neighbors what their mom was cooking for their family. "Pecans," they answered.

So after the children left, Dorothy's mom made up a plate of food and asked Dorothy to deliver it. Dorothy headed off, "filled with the spirit of Christmas," and knocked on the front door. "My Momma fixed you a plate of food for Christmas," she called out. The neighbor peeked out from behind the sheet that covered the window and ordered Dorothy to bring it to the back door. Dorothy walked around to the back door and knocked again. But the woman didn't thank her. She didn't even bother to come to the door. Instead, she just yelled to Dorothy to leave the food on the step. Dorothy was furious at being treated so disrespectfully: "I took a couple of steps back off the porch and I threw the plate as hard as I could against the back door," she said.

Taking care of neighbors was typical for Dorothy's mom. She was a hard-working woman who cared for her own large family, baked cakes, made clothes, and washed people's laundry. She was also a wonderful singer and composer and a role model for Dorothy. "It was my mother who taught us to stand up to our problems, not only in the world around us but in ourselves," Dorothy said. Lessie taught her children many important lessons, some of which Dorothy later listed in her memoir: *Listen and think before you speak. Treat others as you wish to be treated. If you don't love yourself, you can't love anyone else. Be there for each other.*

Lessie and her twin sister both served in leadership roles in the Mount Olive Primitive Baptist Church community. "There was a lot of church in my life," Dorothy said. It was there that Dorothy learned to sing—something that would become very important for her in the future.

Rural Black children in Georgia had limited access to education in the 1940s. From kindergarten until grade five, Dorothy went to school in a basement room at Charles Trinity AME Church. There was one teacher for all the kids—from little ones right up to the twelfth-grade students. Dorothy would listen to the lessons being taught to the older students, form her own theories and opinions, and discuss her ideas with her classmates.

Growing up in the South, Dorothy lived with a constant awareness of danger. When she was ten, her father was beaten badly and left seriously injured on their doorstep. A white supremacist group called the Ku Klux Klan, or the KKK, was responsible. This group, along with segregationist groups known as the White Citizen's Councils, was to blame for a great deal of violence towards Black people in communities across the South. It was difficult for Dorothy to understand how local white men could work alongside Black men at the mill and then hide behind white robes and do such terrible things to their neighbors and coworkers.

That night, Dorothy prayed that her father would survive, and she vowed to dedicate her life to making the world a better place. Luckily, Ray recovered—and when she was only eleven, Dorothy tried to join a local chapter of the National Association for the Advancement of Colored People, also known as the NAACP. She was told she would need a gown to attend the annual gala, something she couldn't possibly afford.

The organizers might have been trying to discourage her for her own safety; in 1949, belonging to an organization like the NAACP was dangerous.

At this time, schools were segregated. Black students and white students went to separate schools. Dorothy attended a public high school for Black students in Lumpkin, a town of about one thousand people that was over an hour's walk from her home. Despite the efforts of some outstanding Black teachers and principals, the school lacked resources, and the education available to Dorothy was very poor. She later said that her high school diploma gave her the academic skills that white students achieved in seventh grade and that she graduated "with little more than a great basketball record and some good singing and dancing experience."

For a teenager with her fierce intelligence, curiosity, and drive, this was deeply frustrating.

Dorothy had an aunt in Philadelphia, and she knew things were different in the North . . . but first she had to find a way out of Lumpkin. So after she finished high school, she left her family and her home and followed her older sister Julia to the city of Columbus, Georgia. She sang in night clubs and at the army base in nearby Fort Benning. In 1957, at age nineteen, she headed to New York City. She took a job as a live-in maid and continued singing. Her stage name was Jean Myers, and she sang in many piano bars and night clubs—including Harlem's famous Cotton Club. She also began meeting people who shared her desire to make change in the world, and she got involved in the civil rights movement, raising bail money for protesters who had been arrested.

By 1965, Dorothy had two young daughters. She needed childcare, and she knew that many other women did too. She had learned that many kids were left at home alone, or were cared for by other children barely old enough to look after themselves. So Dorothy decided to organize a cooperative day care center on the Upper West Side of Manhattan—and to also offer job training and support for parents. Soon, it became a community hub for political organizing and advocacy. A

feminist named Gloria Steinem wrote a column about
the center for *New York* magazine, and the two women
became friends. Together, they travelled around the
country talking about race, class, and feminism. They
later cofounded *Ms.* magazine and the Women's Action
Alliance, which focused on women's rights and
children's education.

When Dorothy was sixty-five, after many years of
activism, she left her home in Harlem and returned to
the South—but not to retire. She opened a bookstore
called Gateway Books, in North Jacksonville, Florida.
Struck by the poverty in this historically Black
neighborhood, and inspired by Michelle Obama and her
White House garden, Dorothy had an idea: a
community food garden could not only combat hunger,

but also provide jobs and a sense of empowerment for children and adults. So, with support from her old friend Gloria Steinem, she got to work—as always, helping people find ways to be there for each other.

John Lewis

Good Trouble, Necessary Trouble

As a civil rights leader, John Lewis changed the course of history. He spent his life tirelessly and courageously working for justice, never wavering in his belief that to create change, it is necessary to make "good trouble." Growing up, his first act of protest involved applying for a library card.

John Robert Lewis grew up in Pike County,
Alabama. His parents were called Eddie and Willie
Mae, and they first met at church. Most people knew
them as Buddy and Willie, but they called each other
Shorty and Sugarfoot. Eddie was a sharecropper,
working in the fields for local farmers, and Willie often
picked cotton alongside her husband, earning fifty cents
a day. John was born on February 21, 1940, in their
small, rented house, with his great-grandmother Bessie
acting as midwife. He was the third child in what would
eventually become a family with ten kids.

When John was four, his family moved to a farm half
a mile away. His parents had bought it for $300—every
penny they had. There were fields of cotton, corn, and
peanuts, and a large house with a front porch sheltered
by a pecan tree.

John described the world of his early childhood as small and safe, surrounded by family. "We were poor—dirt poor," he said, "but I didn't realize it." In a garden behind the house, they grew everything from peas and potatoes to tomatoes and turnips. His mom made delicious, sweet juice from wild grapes and baked pies and cobblers from peaches, pears, and berries. The only thing they didn't eat were the pecans, which they called "Nasty Jennies." These were so bitter that not even the hogs would touch them.

Yum!

Some of John's earliest memories were of taking baths in a tin tub barely big enough to sit in, evenings spent listening to music on the radio, and visits from what they called the "rolling store man," who would drive by with a truck full of goods. When the kids heard his truck coming, they'd gather their coins and run out to buy a Moon Pie or a Coke or an Orange Crush.

On Sundays, they went to church. John loved the festive atmosphere and the singing. After the service, his family would gather at the home of his great-grandparents, whom he called Grandma Bessie and Grandpa Frank. One of Grandma Bessie's hens laid eggs in the hollow of a tree trunk, ten feet off the ground, and it was John's job to scramble up to fetch them. He loved doing this, so his parents put him in charge of looking after the sixty chickens that lived in a henhouse behind their home. He was only five, but he took his role seriously. "I felt as if I had been trusted to care for God's chosen creatures," he said.

Before he fed the hens their breakfast each morning, he talked to them. "I'd speak softly, gently, as if I were hushing a crying baby, and very quickly the cackling would subside, until finally the shed was as silent as a sanctuary." John gave the chickens names, and when one died, he held a funeral, using an old lard can as a coffin, placing flowers by the grave, and delivering a eulogy. After seeing him perform one of these funerals and lead other children in a procession to his chicken cemetery, his family began calling him Preacher. John even tried baptizing his baby chicks. "I was truly intent on saving the little birds' souls," he said.

When John turned six, his parents expected him to begin working with them in the cotton fields. It was hot, backbreaking work—but worse than that, the white landowners made most of the profits. This made John angry, and he made his opinions known—right in the middle of the field. John's brother Adolph got so tired of listening to him that he'd offer to do John's share of the work just to shut him up!

John much preferred school to working in the fields. Wearing his denim overalls, work boots, and his favorite red flannel shirt, he set off each morning on the half-mile hike to the same school his mother had attended: an old building near the church, heated by wood stoves that the students gathered firewood for. John's handwriting was messy, and public speaking terrified him, but his excitement about learning overcame his fears. He especially loved reading biographies of Black people who had made a difference in the world. The first time he left Pike County was for a school field trip to the Tuskegee Institute, where he toured a laboratory just like the one George Washington Carver had worked in.

In the 1940s, Black and white people lived separately in America's South. The system that kept Black people and white people apart—and discriminated against Black people—was called segregation. When John was six, he visited the nearby town of Troy with his father, and he saw this for himself. The washrooms and drinking fountains for white people were clean and modern, whereas the ones marked COLORED were dirty and rundown. At the drug store, he and his father could buy a Coca-Cola, but they weren't allowed to sit at the counter to drink it. And there was a public library that he wasn't allowed to enter. "Even an eight-year-old could see that there was something terribly wrong about that," John said.

John heard that things were different in the North. He heard about schools where Black and white children learned together, and shops where Black and white people could share a lunch counter. He daydreamed about it while he was working in the fields. He and his cousin Della Mae even talked about cutting down a tree and building a bus to take them north.

Then, when he was eleven, something exciting happened. His Uncle Otis—his mother's brother, who was a teacher and a school principal—had always taken a special interest in John. Otis had a feeling that his nephew was destined for a life different from his parents, and he planned a special trip north for the two of them. They loaded up the car with food and drove all the way to Buffalo, New York, to spend the summer with relatives.

John couldn't believe the contrast between this bustling city and his home in Pike County. "It was so busy, almost frantic, the avenues filled with cars, the sidewalks crowded with people, black and white alike, mixing together as if it was the most natural thing in the world," he recalled. He went to a department store, where he rode an escalator for the first time—he hadn't even known that such a thing existed! And he was amazed by the candy counter: "It was like magic, standing there and beholding the variety of sweets laid out behind that glass."

By the end of August, John was happy to return home to his family, but the trip had changed him. He was angry about the racism that surrounded him in Alabama, about the fact that white children went to new, modern schools with playgrounds, while he and his friends started middle school in small cinder block buildings with only dirt fields to play in. Still, he was determined to learn as much as he could.

John's parents valued education too, but they needed his help in the fields and often asked him to stay home and work. John would hide under the porch—and then, when the school bus pulled up, he would run out, jump on the bus, and go to school before they could stop him.

His parents scolded him, but John did it over and over again. "I was going to school, no matter what," he said.

He knew he didn't want to be a farmer. He thought maybe he could be a preacher or a lawyer. "I was obsessed with learning all I could about the world beyond the one I knew," he recalled, "and that's why the school library became like a second home for me."

In 1954, John was in his first year of high school when the US Supreme Court ruled that segregated schools were unconstitutional. He thought everything would change. But instead, state politicians announced that they were going to defy the ruling. White supremacist groups began marching, making threats, and attacking Black men. John's parents wanted him to be careful and stay out of trouble, but he was glad things were getting "stirred up a little bit." The next fall, though, his school was still segregated as if the Supreme Court decision hadn't even happened.

Then, in early 1955, John heard a sermon on the radio that changed his life. It was Martin Luther King Jr. speaking from Montgomery, the capital of Alabama, just fifty miles away. "He was giving voice to everything I'd been feeling and fighting to figure out," John said. That December, Rosa Parks refused to give up her seat on the bus in Montgomery and was arrested, and Martin Luther King Jr. called for Black people to boycott the buses in response. Over the next few months, John followed the news closely. The

Montgomery bus boycott was about fighting back, but it was nonviolent, "a different way of fighting." To John, it felt deeply right.

He wanted to take action. He went to the Pike County public library and requested a library card. He knew the answer would be no, and it was. So he wrote a petition demanding that the library be opened to Black people. It was John's first formal act of protest.

I would like a library card!

Later, as a university student in Tennessee, John became chairman of a civil rights group called the Student Nonviolent Coordinating Committee. He organized sit-ins at segregated lunch counters in Nashville and took part in nonviolent protests. He was arrested and jailed many times for his activism. To create change, he said, you had to get in trouble—"good trouble, necessary trouble."

In 1961, he became one of the first group of Freedom Riders. These were civil rights activists, both Black and white, who travelled by bus through the American South to protest segregation. The US Supreme Court had ruled that racial segregation was not allowed in waiting areas and restaurants at bus terminals, but the southern states ignored this ruling. So, as the Freedom Riders travelled together from state to state, they attempted to enter these spaces designated as white only. They faced arrest, police brutality, and often terrible violence from white protestors as well. But they also drew international attention to the civil rights movement.

Alongside Martin Luther King Jr. and other civil rights leaders, John helped organize the 1963 March on Washington, where he was the youngest speaker. In 1965, he led the first voting rights march from Selma, Alabama, to Montgomery. Six hundred peaceful marchers set out on the fifty-four mile route, but they didn't get far; only six blocks into the march, white police officers attacked the group with night sticks and tear gas as they attempted to cross the Edmund Pettus Bridge. Many of the marchers were beaten, and some very seriously injured. John spent three days in the hospital with a fractured skull. The horrific violence was shown on television, and many Americans were outraged. The day became known as Bloody Sunday.

But that march, which was followed by many others, represented an important turning point in the civil rights movement. John's efforts helped lead to the Civil Rights Act of 1964 and the Voting Rights Act of 1965. And he kept marching, protesting, and speaking up throughout his life. In 2020, at the age of 80, John marched once more across the bridge in Selma to commemorate the fifty-fifth anniversary of that first march. "On this bridge some of us gave a little blood to help redeem the soul of America. Our country is a better country. We are a better people, but we have still a distance to travel to go before we get there," he said.

John Lewis also fought for change in another way: in 1986 he was elected to Congress. He served seventeen terms in the US House of Representatives, became one of the leaders of the Democratic party, and was awarded the Presidential Medal of Freedom. He worked tirelessly until his death in 2020, fighting for voting rights, health care reform, immigration, gun control, and more. His National Book Award–winning graphic novel series, March, continues to be used in schools across the country, helping a new generation of young activists learn about the civil rights movement—and about the importance of making "good trouble."

Anti-Asian racism in North America isn't new; its roots go back centuries. But when the COVID-19 pandemic began, there was a surge in attacks on Asian American and Pacific Islander (AAPI) people. Asian American activists came together to form an organization called Stop AAPI Hate—and young people stepped up to fight back.

One of them was thirteen-year-old fashion designer **Ashley So**, who had spent the early days of the pandemic sewing one thousand face masks. When the attacks started, Ashley was scared for her elderly grandmother. "These attacks are targeting the most vulnerable in our community," she said.

She organized a Stand for Asians rally in San Mateo, California, and hundreds of people came. Since then, Ashley has spoken at numerous demonstrations in the Bay Area. She has also started a petition for Asian American history to be included in textbooks and classrooms—because, she believes, stopping hate starts with education.

Patrisse Cullors

Our History in the Nation

Artist and activist Patrisse Cullors is best known as one of the founders of the Black Lives Matter movement. As a child, she grew up in poverty, witnessing her brothers being harassed and mistreated by police officers—and she began teaching others about the history of racism in America when she was in fourth grade.

Patrisse was born on June 20, 1983, and grew up in Van Nuys, a neighborhood in the San Fernando Valley region of Los Angeles. Her mother, Cherice Simpson, came from a middle-class family of devout Jehovah's Witnesses, but she did not have their support: she had been estranged from them since she was a teenager. Cherice's partner, Alton, was a mechanic. They had four kids: two boys named Paul and Monte, then Patrisse, and finally the baby of the family, Jasmine. Alton was a caring and affectionate father. Patrisse said that even three decades later, the smell of cars and gasoline made her think of "love and snuggles and safety." But he and Cherice didn't always get along, and by the time Patrisse turned six, he had moved out. Still, even though they lived apart, Alton continued to be an important part of Patrisse's life.

Van Nuys was a multiracial, working class neighborhood. Patrisse lived in an apartment building surrounded by constantly changing neighbors. It was, she wrote, "a neighborhood designed to be transient, not a place where roots are meant to take hold." The building had a rundown pool where she learned to swim, but there were no parks or green spaces nearby, and no grocery store. The only places to buy food were the 7-Eleven and a handful of fast-food restaurants.

Patrisse's mother held down two or three different jobs at a time. She worked as a telemarketer, a receptionist, an office cleaner—but none of her jobs paid well. Sometimes their family didn't have enough to eat. For a year, they had no refrigerator, and the kids poured water on their Cheerios instead of milk. Patrisse said they often would've gone hungry if it weren't for the free breakfast and lunch program at their school.

Cherice worked long hours, so Paul, as the oldest, assumed responsibility for Monte, Patrisse, and Jasmine. He woke them in the morning, reminded them to brush their teeth, and helped them get ready for school. He made them grilled cheese sandwiches for dinner, and at night, he told them when it was time to go to bed.

Patrisse loved Paul, but it was Monte who was her playmate. He had a "ginormous heart," Patrisse said. He fed stray cats and dogs and rescued baby birds that had fallen from their nests. At night, the two would watch TV together. Their favorite show was *Beverley Hills, 90210*, which Patrisse described as showing "a world of rich white kids and their problems"—a world where families like hers, with problems like theirs, didn't exist.

In her own neighborhood, the police were constantly driving around. Patrisse sensed that they were not there to help and that they didn't like the people who lived in her part of town. When she was nine, police officers had even raided her apartment, bursting in wearing riot gear to look for her uncle. Patrisse and Jasmine were shouted at and told to stay on the couch while the police searched every corner. "Did they think my uncle was hiding in the dresser drawer?" Patrisse wondered.

There were no playgrounds or community centers in the neighborhood, so Paul and Monte hung out in the alley with their friends. Patrisse liked to follow them around, but they didn't always want their little sister tagging along. One day, the police pulled up, sirens wailing. The boys weren't doing anything wrong, but the police swore at them, pushed them against a wall, and searched them roughly. Patrisse watched, shocked and frozen with fear.

This kind of police harassment and violence toward Patrisse's brothers happened again and again. Finally, their mother moved the family to another part of the neighborhood, but it didn't help. It didn't seem that there were any safe places for the boys.

One place Patrisse did feel safe was at her elementary school. She loved it—and her fourth-grade teacher, Ms. Goldberg, took a special interest in her. She gave Patrisse a book called *The Gold Cadillac*, a story about a girl and her father driving through the southern states in 1950, a time when racial segregation and discrimination were legal and violence toward Black people was a constant threat. Although the story was set forty years earlier, Patrisse related strongly to the terror the characters felt. She understood the connection between that history and the fear she felt in her neighborhood.

Patrisse asked Ms. Goldberg for more books, and she kept reading. She later described these books as "child-size bites of the fight for freedom and justice." Then Patrisse asked her teacher, "Please can I teach the class about the books?" Ms. Goldberg said yes, and

Patrisse prepared presentations for her classmates. She even gave out candy as a reward for students who answered her questions! "I wanted them to know our history in this nation," she said.

When Patrisse was accepted to Millikan Middle School as part of an arts program for gifted children, she was excited. The school was in Sherman Oaks—a wealthy, mostly white neighborhood with big houses and landscaped lawns. Patrisse couldn't get there by bus, so her mom borrowed a car from their neighbor. On the first day, Patrisse was happy to be driven to school. But then she saw the other kids getting out of cars that were shiny and new—and suddenly their neighbor's battered, old station wagon, with missing windows covered by plastic, felt embarrassing. She started asking her mom to drop her off a few blocks away from the school.

Patrisse didn't fit in at Millikan Middle School and her grades dropped. School used to be a place where she felt loved and valued, but at her new school she began to feel that she did not matter. The year that she was twelve, she later wrote, "was the year that I learned that being Black and poor defined me more than being bright and hopeful and ready."

It was around this time that Patrisse's mother told her something surprising and confusing; Alton, the biological father of Patrisse's three siblings, was not Patrisse's biological father. Cherice explained that she and Alton had separated for a while after Monte was born and before Jasmine came along. During that time, Cherice had been in a relationship with a man named Gabriel, and he was Patrisse's biological father. "Do you want to meet him?" Cherice asked her.

Patrisse didn't want anything to change. Alton reassured her that he was still her dad and always would be. A month later, Patrisse met Gabriel for the first time. He was kind and affectionate. He had problems with drugs, he explained, but he was in recovery. The following week, Patrisse and her mom celebrated Gabriel's graduation from a drug- and alcohol-treatment program. Gabriel's family was there as well—his mother, two of his brothers, three of his sisters, and his twenty-year-old son. Patrisse suddenly had a whole new family, and they were all excited to meet her. She was happy to get to know them, but she also found it confusing. This new family wasn't family to Paul, Monte, and Jasmine. Patrisse felt like she was two different people: her mother's daughter, and her father's daughter.

With time she grew close to Gabriel, and she began spending weekends with him and his family. She cheered on her dad and her uncles at their baseball games. Gabriel's mother, her Grandma Vina, had long gray hair and a wide smile, and Patrisse loved having Friday night dinners at her house and eating her homemade chicken gumbo.

But when Patrisse was about sixteen, Gabriel was sent to prison and those happy times came to an end. He wrote to her every week, telling her he missed her. Soon after this, Patrisse's brother Monte also began getting into trouble with the law. He was struggling with serious mental health issues, but instead of receiving treatment and help for his medical condition, he was put in prison. Luckily, Patrisse had two close friends, Rosa and Carla, who supported her and wrote letters to Monte.

Patrisse's friends also supported her when she came out as bisexual during high school. There was a great deal of homophobia at this time, so it wasn't easy—but at school, a small cluster of queer kids formed a support group of sorts, creating a safe space where Patrisse felt accepted. She had a girlfriend, Cheyenne, whom she loved, and she had the encouragement of her cousin Naomi, who had come out before her.

Patrisse wanted to invite Cheyenne over to her house, but Patrisse's home life was complicated. Recently her family had been evicted with little notice, and Cherice's new fiancé, Bernard, had helped them move into his mother's apartment, where he also lived. They were all spending their nights in sleeping bags on the living room floor, and Patrisse hated it. When her friend Carla was kicked out of her home, the two girls began couch surfing—staying with friends and moving from one home to another. Sometimes they slept in Carla's car.

Their art history teacher, a young Black woman named Donna Hill, came to their rescue. She invited the girls to stay with her while they figured things out. Patrisse ended up staying for two years. During this time, she got involved in community organizing, graduated from high school, and went to the Brotherhood Sisterhood social justice camp, where she met people who shared her passion for social justice and learned more about strategies for making change. She studied religion and philosophy at university and later earned a master's degree in fine arts.

In 2013, a young Black teen in Florida named Trayvon Martin was shot while he walked home from the store. His killer—a white man who lived in the neighborhood—was found not guilty and never punished. Patrisse's friend Alicia Garza wrote a Facebook post reacting to this injustice, and Patrisse responded with a hashtag: #BlackLivesMatter. Over the next few days, the two joined up with a third activist, Opal Tometi, and decided to turn #BlackLivesMatter into a call to action. "I hope it impacts more than we can ever imagine," Patrisse wrote.

And it did. Black Lives Matter grew into a transformational movement. Over the next few years, Black Lives Matter protests helped focus attention on the devastating problems of racism and police brutality—and their deep roots in America's history. By harnessing the power of social media to raise awareness and drive change, Black Lives Matter has inspired a generation and helped create the possibility of a better future.

In 2021, Patrisse stepped down as executive director of Black Lives Matter, but she has continued to fight for racial justice, LGBTQ+ rights, and prison abolition, writing books and producing documentary films to amplify the central messages of the Black Lives Matter movement.

Marley Dias

> ## Black Girl Books

Marley Dias became an activist when she was ten years old, and by thirteen she was a published author. She loved dancing, music, sushi, and hanging out with her friends—but it was her love of reading that launched her campaign for change.

Marley was born in Philadelphia on January 3, 2005, just eleven days after her mother earned her PhD and became Dr. Janice Johnson Dias. Janice grew up in St. Mary, Jamaica, and Marley's father, Scott Nevers, was born in Massachusetts. Both sides of Scott's family came from the Cape Verde islands, off the coast of Senegal in West Africa. Janice and Scott named their baby after the legendary Jamaican musician Bob Marley. When Marley was still very small, she and her family left Philadelphia and moved to West Orange, New Jersey, where they lived with their dog, Philly.

As feminists, Janice and Scott wanted to avoid conforming to traditional gender roles in their family. From the moment their daughter was born, they shared the work of caring for her, feeding her, and, as she got older, taking her to play dates and sports events. They tried to help Marley become a strong, confident person who took pride in her accomplishments; Marley said that they raised her to "think like an adult, laugh like a kid, and have the heart of a lion." When she was a toddler, they would often say, "Good job, Marley," and encourage her to repeat it back. They hoped that as she grew up, she would say this to herself and always feel confident in who she was.

It seemed to work: When Marley was in kindergarten, another girl wrote a note that said, "Marley is ugly and dumb." The girl gave it to Marley's good friend, who laughed and passed it on to Marley. But Marley wasn't upset. "I am not dumb and I am not ugly, so it doesn't bother me, Mommy," she told her mother afterward.

Janice sometimes worried about Marley watching television because of the effect it might have on her self-esteem—so many television shows were full of racist, sexist stereotypes. But instead of banning TV, Janice sat down and watched Marley's favorite shows with her. As they watched together, Janice would point out any problems she saw in the stories and characters on the screen. Marley learned to think critically about the TV shows she was watching.

What is this show about?

Though she enjoyed TV, what Marley really loved were books. She called herself a "total book nerd," and read like she thought and talked—fast! When she was nine, her aunt gave her a copy of *Brown Girl Dreaming* by Jacqueline Woodson. When Marley first tried to read it, she didn't get it. The story is written in verse, and Marley was more used to reading prose than poetry. But a year later, she tried again. She recalled, "it opened up a whole new world to me. A world where modern black girls were the main characters—not invisible, not just the sidekick. . . . A world where black girls' stories truly mattered."

But at school, Marley's book choices were getting narrower. Her fifth-grade class had a required reading list, and all the books on it were classics like *Old Yeller* and *Where the Red Fern Grows*. "There wasn't really any freedom for me to read what I wanted," she remembered.

Sitting in a booth at a diner one night, Marley talked to her mom about how she felt. Between bites of her pancakes—a favorite food, at any time of day—she explained that she thought kids should be able to read books about Black girls. "I'm tired of us not being included, of our stories not being told," she said. "I am *sooo* sick and tired of reading books about white boys and their dogs!"

Her mom looked at her. "What are you going to do about it?" she asked.

The more Marley thought about that question, the more she realized that her frustration was connected to a larger problem. It wasn't just about her own freedom to read what she wanted; it was about fairness and equality. How could kids learn to love reading if they never saw themselves depicted in books? "If we're all equal, then we should all be represented equally," Marley said. "If black girls' stories are missing, then the implication is that they don't matter."

Marley realized there was a problem that needed to be addressed, and she knew she had to step up and work for change. Luckily, she had grown up with parents who valued social justice and believed in taking action. When Marley was five, her mom cofounded the GrassROOTS Community Foundation—a social action organization that supports and empowers people living in poverty, especially women and girls. Marley had taken part in the organization's girls' camp, which taught social activism and helped girls build confidence. Her mom's academic and community work was all about social change, and Marley's grandmother in Jamaica was also deeply committed to her community. "Helping people is a family inheritance," Marley said.

Marley decided she would start a book drive, collect

books where Black girls were the main characters, and donate them to schools. She set a goal of one thousand books—because, she said, "it seemed like an appropriately huge number." She started with a hashtag: #1000BlackGirlBooks. She'd spent enough time watching cat videos on YouTube to know that social media could be extremely powerful! She launched the campaign in the fall of 2015.

Because she was only ten at that time, she didn't have her own social media accounts yet, so her mom helped, making social media posts using the hashtag for her. Marley's two best friends, Briana and Amina, got involved. (They called themselves BAM—for Briana, Amina, and Marley!) The campaign got off to a slow start and, afterward, Marley remembered being worried: "It wasn't really working. I remember it was November, and we almost had 100 books . . . So it was really stressful for me to think, 'How are we going to get more books?'"

Marley was also busy with other things—like visiting the West African country of Ghana. In December 2015, Marley and her mom spent ten days there with an organization called African Health Now. Marley helped at a health fair and she served Christmas dinner to hundreds of orphans. She loved the music and the dancing, and the beautiful fabrics and fashions . . . and eating jollof rice for the first time. "For me as an American-born black person, Africa gave me a new, exciting opportunity to learn," Marley said. "This understanding of and gratitude for my African roots is a gift I'll carry with me forever."

During this trip, she visited a place called Elmina Castle. Built on Ghana's western coast by the Portuguese in 1482, this whitewashed fortress later became a major stop on the transatlantic slave trade route. Thousands of enslaved Africans were imprisoned there before passing through the infamous Door of No Return and being forced onto ships making the dangerous journey to the United States, the Caribbean, or Brazil. It was painful to see, but Marley was glad she went. "[It's] so important to know my history," she said. "I learned so much but cried while I was there, and I sometimes cry thinking about how horribly our ancestors were treated."

After Marley returned home, her book drive started to gain momentum on social media. By February 2016, she had collected seven hundred books—and her campaign went viral. She was invited to go on *The Ellen DeGeneres Show*, where she was given a check for $10,000, plus a laptop to do her own writing. She caught the attention of *Teen Vogue*, *People* magazine, and dozens of other media outlets. That July, Marley was named Editor in Residence of Elle. com, and she interviewed a number of famous people—including the award-winning filmmaker Ava DuVernay, the ballet dancer Misty Copeland, and the politician Hillary Clinton.

Marley soon surpassed her original goal of one thousand books. By 2021, she had collected more than thirteen thousand! She donated books to local schools and to schools in Ghana, and she travelled to Jamaica to donate over one thousand books to the school her mother had attended as a child. She spoke at events across the United States, even making an appearance alongside Michelle Obama and Oprah Winfrey at the White House. "When I speak at events," Marley said, "I often wear my dad's ties and my mom's earrings. It's a small, almost secret way of having them with me when I'm up there onstage, talking to a roomful of strangers. It makes me feel safe."

At thirteen, Marley became an author herself. Her book *Marley Dias Gets It Done (And So Can You!)* is packed with practical advice and inspiring words for other young activists. Two years later, she found another way to promote diverse books; she became a host and executive producer for a Netflix series called *Bookmarks: Celebrating Black Voices.* Whether in movies, television, or literature, Marley believes that Black girls matter and that their stories need to be told. She argues that young readers need to have access to diverse books, so that all kids can find stories that include people like themselves. "In order for us to be the change we wish to see in the world," Marley says, "we must see ourselves first—in fact and in fiction."

THREE

PROTECTING
OUR PLANET

POLITICIANS AND SCIENTISTS, KIDS AND TEENS: * * * from the * * * WHITE HOUSE to the CLASSROOM, THESE KID TRAILBLAZERS MOTIVATED MILLIONS OF PEOPLE around the world to DEFEND THE ENVIRONMENT * and the * LIVES THAT DEPEND ON IT.

David Suzuki

Solace in the Wilderness

Canadian scientist David Suzuki is famous for his radio and television programs about the natural world, and for challenging governments to take action to protect the environment. Today, he is respected as one of Canada's leading environmental activists, but when he was six years old, the Canadian government detained his family and held them as prisoners in their own country.

David Takayoshi Suzuki was born in Vancouver, Canada, on March 24, 1936, as was his twin sister, Marcia. David arrived first, which meant he was considered the younger twin; in the Japanese tradition, the elder twin allows the younger to go first. David was definitely bigger though—at nine pounds, he was three times the size of his sister!

David's grandparents had emigrated from Japan many years earlier, hoping to escape poverty. His mother, Setsu Nakamura, and his father, Carr Suzuki, were born in Vancouver and met while they were working for a local company that imported Japanese food. Employees were not allowed to date, so Carr quit his job. They got married, and two years later, the twins were born, followed by Aiko, and then Dawn.

When David was small, his parents ran a dry-cleaning shop in Vancouver. He recalled, "As a boy I would stand for hours behind a steam operated machine that Dad used to press shirts and pants, asking him a steady stream of questions as he worked. . . . He was my great hero and role model." David loved to go fishing with his father, and one of his earliest memories was of catching little trout in a small lake just outside the city. On other occasions, they drove sixty miles inland, where they would ride horses upstream from the Vedder Canal to camp and fish in the Fraser Valley. "I was always fascinated that we could let the horses go at the end of our ride, and they would find their way home," he remembered.

In the first half of the twentieth century, anti-Asian racism in Canada was intense and widespread. Japanese Canadians were not allowed to vote, and they faced a great deal of prejudice and discrimination. As a young child, though, David knew little of this. That was about to change—and in a way that no one could have foreseen.

In December 1941, when David was five years old, Japan attacked Hawaii's Pearl Harbor. In response, Canada, like the US, declared war on Japan. A few months later, the government passed a law called the War Measures Act. This law took away all the legal rights of Canadians of Japanese descent, who were considered "enemy aliens." David's parents had been born in Canada and had never lived anywhere else, but suddenly they were viewed with suspicion. David explained, "To the white community we looked different; we looked just like the enemy and thus deserved to be treated like the enemy."

Under the War Measures Act, the Canadian government seized the houses and possessions of families like David's. Within months, more than twenty thousand Canadians of Japanese descent who lived on the West Coast were forced from their homes, transported to remote areas in British Columbia's interior, and imprisoned in crudely built camps for the duration of World War II.

David's father had anticipated that something like this could happen. Soon after the attack on Pearl Harbor, he volunteered to work at a road camp where Japanese Canadians were helping to build the Trans-Canada Highway. He had hoped that by volunteering, he would show that he could be trusted, and his family would be left alone.

But in early 1942, David and his mother and siblings were forced to board a train for the long journey out of Vancouver, away from the coast and into the mountains. David was only six, and it didn't occur to him to wonder why everyone on the train was Japanese. "I just played games with Martha Sasaki, whose family was seated next to ours, and we had a delicious time," he recalled. "I can only marvel at how my parents shielded us from the turmoil they must have undergone."

The train ride took David and his family to an internment camp known as Slocan City, in British Columbia's Kootenay region. The town of Slocan City had been built in the 1890s, when people looking for silver poured into the Slocan Valley, but by the 1940s it was a ghost town, the buildings filthy and falling apart. The Suzuki family were placed in a tiny, foul-smelling room in a derelict old hotel. "I had to learn to avoid the hazardous floorboards on the porch that encircled the building," David said. Every morning, he woke up covered with bedbug bites.

At first, there wasn't even a school for the children, but David didn't mind: "I had lots of time to play," he said. He already loved the wilderness and he used his free time to explore the valley. There were rivers and lakes filled with fish, and forests filled with wolves, bears, and deer.

A year later, a school was built about a mile away, and David began first grade. His parents would ask him about what he was learning and listen patiently as he talked about his day. David completed three grades that year, skipping straight from first grade into fourth.

But despite his success at school, he didn't seem happy. When he stopped wanting to go at all, his father, Carr, decided to walk to the school to investigate. As he followed train tracks through the snow, he saw a boy being chased, hit, and kicked by a group of kids—and realized it was his own son.

Hey! Get back here!

Looking back, David remembered being isolated and bullied. Most of the other kids were Nisei, a Japanese term meaning second generation; as children of immigrants, they were born in Canada but their parents had been born in Japan. They spoke both English and Japanese fluently. But David was Sansei, or third generation, and could only speak English.

After the war, David's family was relocated to the nearby town of Kaslo. David felt uncomfortable with the white children at his new school. He'd had white friends before the war, but now everything felt different: "They seemed alien, and I shied away from them," David said. He sought refuge in nature, exploring the lakes and mountains, and taking the steamboat to the head of the lake to watch the salmon returning to spawn.

Then his family moved again, taking the train across the prairies to Ontario. They lived for one year in Olinda, where David and his sister attended school in a one-room schoolhouse, and then moved to the nearby town of Leamington, just across the border from the

American city of Detroit. David's family were the first people of color to move to Leamington, and they were nervous. During the war, anti-Asian propaganda portrayed Japanese people in negative, stereotyped ways, fueling the racism and bigotry that already existed. Painfully, this also affected David's view of himself: "Every time I looked in the mirror, I saw that stereotype," he said.

In ninth grade, David started at Leamington High School. He loved it so much that when his parents moved a hundred miles away, to a Canadian city called London, he stayed behind with friends to finish the year. The family he lived with were Issei—first generation, born in Japan. They spoke Japanese at home, and David learned a little. He also started writing poetry. One poem, which was printed in the school yearbook when he was fourteen, began:

Let us take a walk through the wood,
While we are in this imaginative mood;
Let us observe Nature's guiding hand,
Throughout this scenic, colorful land.

When the school year ended, David joined his family again. His parents had bought some land in London and his uncles, who had lived in the city for years, were helping build a small home on it. When David arrived, the house was only half finished. David started working for his uncles' company, Suzuki Brothers Construction. "I learned enough to frame, make sidewalks, build a fruit cellar, and pour a concrete slab at the entrance to our house," he recalled. Two years later, the house was finally finished. It was a relief for David and his sisters; they were embarrassed to live in a house that was still under construction.

Starting a new high school was hard and lonely. It seemed like everyone at London Central Collegiate already knew each other—and David was so shy that if he saw another student outside school, he would cross the street to avoid having to make conversation. He spent most of his free time exploring a nearby swamp. It was, he said, "a magical place, filled with mystery and an incredible variety of plant and animal life." When David would come home soaking wet and covered in mud, his mother always took an interest in what he had found, from salamander eggs to baby turtles. "She never scolded me but would *ooh* and *ahh* over each little treasure," he recalled.

In David's last year of high school, a friend suggested he should run for school president. David was sure he'd lose, but his father convinced him to try anyway. "How do you know if you don't even try?" he said. And besides, Carr pointed out, there was no shame in losing. To David's shock, he won by a landslide!

David went on to become a professor at the University of British Columbia. He also began teaching science to children on a TV show called *Suzuki on*

Science and started a radio series to raise awareness about the devastating impact humans were having on the earth. Many listeners wrote to David asking what they could do, so he formed the David Suzuki Foundation to empower people to take action in their communities. For more than four decades, David has hosted *The Nature of Things* on CBC television. Broadcast in nearly fifty countries, the show helps people to learn more about the natural world and take action to protect it.

Al Gore

Great
Expectations

Al Gore is a former American vice president—but he is also an author, an environmental activist, and a winner of the Nobel Peace Prize for his work on climate change. He was only six years old when a newspaper headline described him as a budding politician!

Albert Arnold Gore was born in Washington, DC, on March 31, 1948. His father, who was also named Albert Gore, was a US congressman and senator. His mother, Pauline LaFon, was one of the first women to graduate from Vanderbilt University Law School. The couple's first child, Nancy, was ten years old by the time their son was born. They had been hoping for a second child for a long time; Pauline said Albert's birth was "kind of a miracle." They called him Little Al.

He's perfect!

Al's parents both came from poor, hardworking families. His dad, Albert Senior, grew up on a farm near Nashville, Tennessee. He worked his way through college and then attended the Nashville YMCA Night Law School. On his drive home after class, he would stop for coffee at the Andrew Jackson Hotel, and talk to the waitress, Pauline. Like Albert, she was studying law at night. The two graduated together, and a year later, they married. By the time their son was born more than a decade later, Albert was a successful politician. He and Pauline hoped that Little Al would follow in his father's footsteps.

As a young boy, Al lived with his family in suite 809 at the Fairfax Hotel on Embassy Row in Washington, DC. The suite underneath his family's home was occupied by an elderly senator who complained about the noise Al made bouncing his basketball. There was no playground nearby, so when Al invited school friends over they would head to the hotel's flat roof, where they would play with a Frisbee or drop water balloons on cars waiting for the light to change on the street far down below.

Al's parents set very high standards for their son's behavior. His father was particularly demanding, even requiring Al to do fifty push-ups every morning before school! His mother would strategically include Al in dinner conversations with guests that she thought he might learn from. He later recalled, "As I was entering high school, my mother was reading *Silent Spring* and the dinner table conversation was about pesticides and the environment."

Al's childhood was wealthy and privileged, but at times it was also lonely. His parents were often away, and Al was looked after by various babysitters, au pairs, and cousins. Still, he found ways to have fun, such as rearranging all the living room furniture to make forts. Sometimes he would be left in the apartment with his sister, Nancy, and her friend Barbara. The two teenage girls considered Little Al to be a pest, especially when he followed them around singing songs from TV commercials. On top of that, he was a terrible tattletale. "Every time we tried to do something, Al would catch us and say, 'I'm telling! I'm telling! I'm telling Dad!'" Barbara recalled.

The high expectations that Al's parents had for their son were reinforced by the high standards of the school they sent him to. Al attended St. Albans School, a prestigious private Christian school for boys. The sons of Franklin D. Roosevelt, Robert and Ted Kennedy, and George H. W. Bush all attended St. Albans. It was a school that emphasized discipline and structure. The boys wore coats and ties and were required to take part in sports. The school day often ended as late as six o'clock.

Every year, Al looked forward to school finishing so he could go to Tennessee, where he spent his summers on his family's farm—and where, when he was about eleven, he began hanging out with a group of local teens. They called themselves the Snow Creek Gang. Two years later, he met a girl named Donna—the older sister of one of his friends—and the two began dating. They spent the next few summers together, playing basketball, swimming in the river, and walking in the woods.

But despite some good times, summers were far from a vacation for Al. He was up at the crack of dawn, working with the farmhands, tending the livestock, growing and harvesting tobacco, and clearing dense brush.

When Al was fourteen, he got his driver's license. Although he was generally a careful and controlled person, he was not a cautious driver. "He was constantly running us into hog feeders and running us off the road," one of his friends said. One time, he tried to pass a truck on a narrow stretch of road and ended up in the ditch—upside down! The impact was so hard that Al's shoes flew off his feet. Luckily, he wasn't badly hurt . . . but it was the end of his father's Chevy.

In his senior year, Al boarded at St. Albans School, despite it being located close to his home. The boys would compete to see who could sleep latest and still make it to morning chapel on time. They all used clip-on ties to make dressing quicker, but Al went even further; he cut the back of his dress shirt open so he could slip it on without having to do up the buttons! "He took off his jacket in lineup and showed us his bare back," one of his classmates recalled. Al also took advantage of any opportunity to nap and showed up for dinner with pillow creases on his face so often that the other students started referring to those creases as "Gore's disease."

Rather than dedicating himself to one overwhelming passion, Al was good at almost everything in school. In his high school yearbook, the editors included a drawing of Al as a statue on a pedestal—holding a football, a basketball, and a discus. The caption read "People who have no weaknesses are terrible."

After he graduated from high school, Al was accepted to Harvard. On his second day on campus, he began a campaign to become the student council president, which succeeded. But he wasn't sure about his future. At first, he thought he might study English and be a novelist. He also loved science, and one class he took sparked his interest in climate change. The course was taught by a professor named Roger Revelle, who was one of the first scientists to study global warming and to measure the rising levels of carbon dioxide in our planet's atmosphere.

Al also studied religion, worked at a newspaper, and considered being a journalist. In the end, though, he followed in his father's footsteps. When his father sold Al a farm in the district that Albert had represented, Al decided to quit law school and campaign for an available seat in Congress. He won, joining the US House of Representatives in 1976. Al Gore was one of the first US politicians to understand the threat posed by climate change. He held the first congressional hearings on climate change, and he spoke publicly about this issue throughout the 1980s.

Al Gore went on to serve two terms as vice president, from 1993 to 2001, using his position to promote environmental initiatives. He has given talks around the world, written books, and starred in the documentary film *An Inconvenient Truth.* In 2007, he was awarded the Nobel Peace Prize for his efforts to educate about and take action against climate change.

In the fall of 2021, Al spoke at the United Nations Climate Change Conference—known as COP26—in Glasgow, Scotland. "It has never been more important to hold our leaders accountable to their words and pledges," he said. "Advocates for climate action cannot—and must not—let up."

Greta Thunberg

School Strike
for Climate

Greta Thunberg is a young environmental activist from Sweden. She challenges world leaders to take action on climate change and has inspired millions of students to walk out of their schools and join the fight for our planet. But when she started her first school strike, Greta felt very much alone.

Greta's mother, Malena Ernman, was a successful opera singer. Her father, Svante Thunberg, was an actor. In a remarkable coincidence, he was also a descendant of Svante Arrhenius, a physicist who won the Nobel Prize a hundred years before Greta was born for his work exploring how carbon dioxide is warming our planet.

Before they had children, Malena sang at opera houses all over Europe and Svante worked at three theater companies. They were often in different countries as they pursued their separate careers, and they knew something would have to change if they wanted to have a family. Together, they decided that Malena would continue her work and that Svante would stay home with the kids.

Greta was born on January 3, 2003, in Stockholm, Sweden. When she was very young, the family traveled and Malena sang. For two months at a time, they lived in Berlin, Paris, Vienna, Amsterdam, and Barcelona. They spent summers in Austria or France or England. When Greta was three, her sister, Beata, was born. Malena and Svante bought a large car, so that when they moved they could take the kids' tricycles, doll houses, and other toys with them. Sometimes Greta's grandmother Mona came to stay with them, but mostly it was just their family of four. The family was close and enjoyed spending time together.

When Greta was seven, she began attending Franska Skolan, a private school in Stockholm. The following year, she began having trouble at home and at school. "She cried at night when she should be sleeping. She cried on her way to school. She cried in her classes and during her breaks," her mother later wrote. Almost every day, her parents received a phone call from the school and her father would have to pick her up. Greta had a dog she loved—a golden retriever named Moses—and she spent hours with him, stroking his fur. Her parents tried to understand what was wrong but nothing they did seemed to help. Greta wouldn't talk to anyone outside her family. She stopped doing the things she loved, like playing the piano. She stopped laughing. And then she stopped eating.

Malena decided that the family needed to focus on getting Greta well, so she took a break from traveling. She and Svante took Greta to appointments with doctors and psychologists to seek answers, and they found support from an eating disorders clinic. Greta was malnourished; she had no energy and was depressed. At school, Greta was quiet and withdrawn—and she often didn't go at all. Her teacher, Anita von Berens, began to give Greta lessons during breaks and free periods in the library.

Although being at school was difficult for Greta, learning was not. She had a photographic memory; she only had to see something once and she would remember it. She could list the capital of every country in the world and every element in the periodic table. Her father, Svante, was a bit like her; when he was a child, he collected and memorized airline timetables.

Greta wanted to feel better, but recovering from her depression and her trouble with eating was not easy.

"Am I going to get well again?" she asked. "Of course you are," her mom told her. "When am I going to get well?" Greta asked. "Soon," her mother said. But Malena didn't really know, because she still didn't understand what was wrong. It was a scary time for the whole family.

Luckily, Greta had lots of support. She began taking medication to help with her depression, and she started to talk to her parents about the terrible bullying she had been experiencing at school. The doctors explained that Greta was autistic, and that she also had an anxiety disorder. With time, understanding, and treatment, Greta began feeling better. Her teacher, Anita, kept on helping her through sixth, seventh, and eighth grade.

As Greta continued to recover, she and her sister Beata learned about the refugee crisis. They persuaded their parents to support a Syrian family seeking asylum in Sweden. Greta was also becoming increasingly focused on what would become her central passion: the environment.

Later, Greta said that her worries about climate change had been one of the things that contributed to her depression. Greta's class had watched a film about the huge amount of plastic garbage floating in the South Pacific Ocean. Afterward, Greta had been deeply worried by what she had seen, but other students were talking about shopping and vacations overseas and eating hamburgers for lunch—all things that were bad for the environment! She couldn't understand why no one around her seemed to be as concerned as she was, and this made her feel very hopeless and alone.

What helped, Greta said, was taking action. She began advocating for change at home first, persuading her parents to reduce their carbon footprint. The family stopped eating meat, and when Greta was thirteen, her mother agreed to stop flying, giving up her career as an opera singer.

Then, in May 2018, Greta won a climate change writing contest, and her essay was published in a Swedish newspaper. Another activist read it and reached out to her, and Greta had a few phone meetings with his youth group, brainstorming strategies to bring attention to the climate crisis. When Greta heard about some American students who had organized a national school walkout to protest gun violence, she was inspired—but the other young activists were focused on different plans.

So, in August 2018, Greta told her parents that she was going on strike to put pressure on the Swedish government. She rode her bike to the Swedish Parliament buildings and sat outside, holding up a sign reading SKOLSTREJK FÖR KLIMATET—in English, School Strike for Climate. The first day, she was alone. But a few journalists reported her story, and Greta posted on social media, and soon others started to join her.

Greta announced she would continue striking every Friday until Sweden met the goals of the Paris Agreement—an international treaty to reduce greenhouse gas emissions and limit the warming of the planet. The number of people joining her grew. All across Europe, students started similar protests in their own communities. That fall, Greta gave a TED Talk that has been viewed by millions around the world. In December 2018, she spoke at the United Nations Climate Change Conference in Poland—and her speech went viral.

By this time, thousands of children were skipping school on Fridays to demand that their governments take action. Greta's demonstration had sparked a movement known as Fridays for Future, Youth Strike for Climate, or simply Climate Strike.

On March 15, 2019, less than a year after Greta's first day of striking, more than a million students participated in strikes around the world. Two months later, the students organized another global strike, and children and teenagers in more than 150 countries took part. In September, the largest global climate strike ever took place—in one week, over 6 million people protested in more than 4,500 separate locations! In Brazil, China, India, Mexico, the US, and other countries, young people organized events, led protests, and demanded change.

Greta saw an opportunity to make a difference for the planet's future, so she decided to take a year off from school to focus on activism. She traveled from Europe to the United States—by sailboat, to avoid flying—and spoke at the UN Climate Change Action Summit, in New York City. "This is all wrong," she said in her speech. "I shouldn't be up here. I should be back in school on the other side of the ocean. Yet you all come to us young people for hope? How dare you!"

Greta has received numerous awards for her activism. She was *Time* magazine's Person of the Year in 2019, and she has been nominated for the Nobel Peace Prize three times. Her courage, her single-minded focus on science, her unwillingness to tolerate hypocrisy, and her refusal to be intimidated by critics have helped inspire a worldwide movement. We are facing a crisis, Greta says, and to do that, we need people who think differently. Greta says that being autistic is one of the things that has helped her achieve her goals. "That means I'm sometimes a bit different from the norm," she says. "And given the right circumstances—being different is a superpower."

Mari Copeny

Fighting for Flint Kids

Mari Copeny is best known for her work raising awareness about the water crisis in her city of Flint, Michigan. She is passionate about helping her community—especially other kids—and although she's still too young to vote, she plans to run for president in 2044!

Mari was born on July 6, 2007, and lives with her family: her mother, Loui (aka Lulu) Brezzell; her dad, Chez; her older sister, Blair; and her younger brother and sister. Mari's full name is Amariyanna Copeny, but she is also known as Little Miss Flint—a title she won at a beauty pageant in 2015.

Mari grew up in a family that believed in helping others. From the time she was a toddler, she volunteered at food banks with her grandmother, and around the holidays she helped her mother fill boxes with items for families in need. So when Mari won the Little Miss Flint title, she started thinking about how she could use it to make a difference. One of her goals at that time was to help create a better relationship with the police in her community so that kids wouldn't have to be afraid of them.

Mari first made national headlines when she was just eight years old. The year was 2016, Barack Obama was president, and Flint, Michigan, was dealing with a water crisis. Two years earlier, to save money, Michigan officials had switched Flint's water supply from Lake Huron and the Detroit River to the Flint River. Mari and her little sister Keilani broke out in strange rashes. The family didn't know what was causing them—maybe it was the soap they were using, Lulu thought. But then they found out that the problem was the water coming out of their taps. It hadn't been properly treated to kill bacteria, as tap water usually is. The water also had dangerously high levels of lead leaching from the city's aging lead pipes. Many people were getting sick. The water wasn't safe to drink, or even to bathe in. "It smelled funny, and it was brown," Mari said.

Mari wanted to do something to help the people in her community. "When the water crisis began, all I wanted to do was to fight for my younger siblings, especially my little sister, who would get such bad rashes from the water that she would need to be covered in a special ointment and wrapped in plastic wrap to try to help heal her skin," she recalled. "I wanted to fight for all the kids here that were scared and confused. I wanted to fight for the adults that had to teach the kids that the water was poison. Back in the beginning, nobody believed that anyone would listen to me, not even my mom. After all, I was just an eight-year-old kid. But I knew I had to keep fighting, keep speaking, keep trying until someone listened."

Mari had competed in more than fifty beauty pageants by the time she was in third grade, and she saw an opportunity to use her Little Miss Flint title to help her community. She went to meetings and rallies, and like many people from Flint, her family planned to travel to Washington, DC, to watch the congressional hearings about the crisis in their community. Before the trip, Mari decided to write to President Obama. She explained that she was one of the children affected by the unsafe water and asked for his help. "I've been doing my best to march in protest and to speak out for all the kids that live here in Flint," she wrote. "My mom said chances are you will be too busy with more important things, but there is a lot of people coming on these buses and even just a meeting from you or your wife would really lift people's spirits."

And to her amazement, Obama wrote back! He announced his decision to visit Flint by publicly sharing his letter to Mari. "You're right that Presidents are often busy, but the truth is, in America, there is no more important title than citizen," he wrote. "Letters from kids like you are what make me so optimistic for the future."

People across the United States read the letters— and back in Flint, Mari could hardly wait to meet the president. On the big day, she dressed up for the occasion, wearing her purple Little Miss Flint sash. When she saw President Obama, she ran toward him, and he lifted her up for a hug. "You know, I wrote to you!" she said. "I know! That's why I decided to come," he told her.

"I didn't expect anything when I sent the letter. I didn't even think he would write back," Mari said later. "I thought I was being pranked when I heard he wanted to meet me. But it was the greatest, awesomest, most epic experience of my life."

Mari's letter and President Obama's visit to Flint helped raise awareness nationwide. A state of emergency was declared and Obama authorized $100 million to be spent to help address the water crisis. And something else important had happened: Mari had discovered the power of speaking up for change.

She decided to do something to support other kids in Flint. She began fundraising to put together backpacks that included everything local children would need for school that fall: pens and pencils, markers and crayons, notebooks, highlighters, and more. Although she raised enough money to give away one hundred backpacks, she was sad that she couldn't help more kids. So the following summer, just after she turned ten, she launched a new fundraising campaign—and this time, she raised enough money to fill one thousand backpacks! "Education is everything, especially when dealing with kids who have had to live with the water crisis in Flint," Mari said. "A good education can help Flint kids to change the world."

In January 2017, Mari became a national youth ambassador to the Women's March on Washington. A few months later she addressed a large crowd at a rally in front of the White House, criticizing then president Donald Trump for failing to keep his promises to fix Flint's problems and speaking out against his immigration policies as well.

By the time she was twelve, Mari was losing interest in pageants: "I'm kind of too old to be wearing a crown and sash around, traveling around. That's just a little bit baby-ish," she said. Besides, she was busy: Flint still didn't have safe water, so Mari raised enough money to buy over 200,000 bottles of water for people in her city. Her activism was also extending past Flint's borders into other communities where water had also been contaminated, and she was starting to focus on a wider range of issues.

By the time she was fourteen, Mari had worked against bullying, spoken twice at the March for Science, raised over $500,000 to support various projects for the children of Flint, organized a yearly Christmas event that has given away thousands of toys, arranged movie screenings for local kids, and started a book project to provide books written by authors of color to local young readers. She started the Dear Flint Kids project, encouraging people from around the world to send messages of support to children in Flint, and received thousands of letters in response.

Mari also raised enough money to distribute more than a million bottles of safe drinking water. These were badly needed, but Mari knew that single-use plastic bottles were not good for the environment. So she teamed up with a company making water filters and began raising money to provide these filters to people who needed them.

Mari has encouraged other kids to speak up about what matters to them and to help their communities. "You don't have to run big fundraisers," she said. "You can help a neighbor carry in groceries, pick up trash in your neighborhood, read books to little kids, and other easy things like that."

So who inspired Mari? She had many strong role models—like Martin Luther King Jr. and his daughter,

Dr. Bernice King, as well as Barack Obama, actress and activist Yara Shahidi, and her own big sister, Blair.

Mari has plenty of regular kid interests. She loves reading comic books, cheerleading, tap dancing, watching anime, and drawing. She likes hanging out with her friends—and she says they all love to eat!

But she dreams big. "Obama was once a Black kid with a dream, and he was able to achieve it, so I can, too," she says. "When I'm president, I'll make sure I use my voice to speak for the people—especially kids."

Around the world, young people are demanding action on the climate crisis. One of them is Uganda's **Vanessa Nakate**. In 2019, she began protesting, alone, outside Uganda's parliament building. "They keep talking about climate change being a matter of the future, but they forget that people of the Global South, it is a matter of now," she said. "Literally, in my county, a lack of rain means starvation and death for the less privileged."

Using social media, Vanessa founded Youth for Future Africa and the Rise Up Climate Movement. She led a campaign to save the Congo rainforest, which she called "the lungs of Africa," and she started the Green Schools Project to help schools in Uganda transition to using solar energy. She has spoken at international conferences, urging world leaders to take action. Vanessa is also working against racism, using her platform to demand that marginalized and Indigenous voices be included in the environmental movement.

FOUR

HARNESSING THE POWER OF ART

✳ ✳ FROM ✳ ✳

POETRY

✳ TO ✳

NETFLIX,

═══ THESE ═══

KID TRAILBLAZERS

═══ USED ═══

WORDS, IMAGES,

AND STORIES

TO WORK FOR CHANGE
and used their platforms
to advocate for a

BETTER WORLD.

Audre Lorde

The Power of Words

Audre Lorde was a writer, librarian, and civil rights activist—and in her own words, "black, lesbian, mother, warrior, poet." Throughout her life she used her creativity to fight injustice—and she discovered the power of poetry at a very early age.

Audre's mother, Linda Gertrude Belmar, was from the Caribbean country of Grenada. Her father, Frederick Byron Lorde, was originally from Barbados. A year after they married, they sold everything they owned and immigrated to the United States. They arrived in Harlem in 1924.

Around this time, millions of immigrants were coming to the US. Most were young, poor, and hopeful about the opportunities they would find in their new country. However, there was a lot of prejudice against immigrants—and especially immigrants who were Black. Linda and Byron found jobs, and Byron took night classes to become a real estate agent—but their new life was harder than they'd imagined, and Linda missed her home in Grenada.

Five years after they arrived in the United States, Linda and Byron, still living in Harlem, had their first child—a girl named Phyllis. Two years later, Helen was born, and then on February 18, 1934, the baby of the family arrived. They named her Audrey Geraldine Lorde.

Audrey's parents cared about their children and wanted them to succeed, but they had rigid ideas about how kids should be raised. They thought children should be seen and not heard, and they expected their daughters to obey them without question. Although they worked hard to provide their daughters with food, shelter, and education, they were not affectionate toward them. Their style of parenting was not a good fit for their youngest child, and Audrey often felt unloved.

To make matters worse, she felt excluded and mistreated by her sisters, who were close in age and shared a room. The three girls were often left alone, and Phyllis and Helen were expected to take care of their younger sister—but it wasn't easy! Audrey was stubborn and demanding, and she had terrible tantrums. Later, Phyllis and Helen said that Audrey was the family favorite. She didn't have to do chores, and she was the only one who dared to stand up to their parents.

But Audrey didn't feel like she was anyone's favorite. She didn't speak until she was four and she struggled with a stutter. She had problems with her feet and had to wear special orthopedic shoes. She also had very poor eyesight and needed glasses. "Until I got spectacles when I was four I thought trees were green clouds," she later recalled.

Audrey was not allowed to go outside to play. Her mother still missed her home in the Caribbean and felt unsafe in Harlem, and she didn't like to let the children out of her sight. Most of Audrey's time was spent with her mother and her two aunts. She went to the market with her mom to buy Caribbean produce and she listened to her stories about Grenada: the food and the fruit, the hills and the beautiful sea.

Audrey learned to read at the same time she learned to speak, at age four. When she was five, she began going to Saint Mark's Academy Elementary School. Her sisters had been students there before her and had been obedient and well-behaved. Audrey, however, was different. She argued with the nuns and she questioned religious ideas that she was expected to accept as truth. On top of that, she was left-handed, which at the time was frowned upon, and she liked to do things her own way. She even started writing her name as Audre instead of Audrey because she didn't like how the letter *y* looked. The nuns, shocked that she was so different from her sisters, punished Audre for disobedience. They sent notes home—where she was then punished by her mother as well.

In the summer of 1945, when Audre was eleven, the family moved to Upper Harlem and rented an apartment in Washington Heights. It was a white working-class neighborhood, and Audre's family was the first Black family to move to the block. Audre's parents discouraged friendships with other children and did not allow the girls to have friends over, but in this new part of town Audre was given more freedom to go outside to play and jump rope.

From sixth grade to eighth grade, Audre attended Saint Catherine's School, which was just one block from her home. Audre was the school's first Black student and the other children made fun of her braids and left mean notes in her desk. Audre had so many emotions building up inside, but she had always found it hard to talk about how she felt—and so she turned to poetry.

At their father's political meetings, or at their aunts' homes, Phyllis or Helen would play piano and Audre would recite poems; their parents liked to show off their daughters' skills. By the time Audre was twelve, she had memorized many poems. "Words had an energy and power and I came to respect that power early," she recalled. If someone asked how she was feeling, Audre would often reply with poetry: "I would recite a poem and somewhere in that poem would be the feeling. . . . It might be a line, it might be an image." As she got older, it was hard to find poems to express all the things she felt. "There were so many complex emotions, it seemed, for which poems did not exist," she said. She began creating her own poems, in secret.

After two years at Saint Catherine's School, Audre was accepted to Hunter High School, a small school for girls who excelled academically. She became involved with the school's literary magazine and threw herself into the world of poetry, studying Keats, T. S. Eliot, and Edna St. Vincent Millay. And she finally made real friends.

Although she was the only Black girl in the group, most of these teens were also children of immigrants and they had many things in common. Together they skipped classes and visited bookstores. They held seances and tried to summon the ghosts of long dead poets. They read their poems aloud to each other. They called themselves "The Branded." After years of writing poems in secret, Audre finally had a writing community.

At home, though, she was deeply unhappy. Much of her sadness came from her difficult relationship with her mother and her sisters. She didn't talk about those feelings with her friends, but she wrote about them in her journal. "Last year was rotten," she wrote. "Maybe this year I'll get along a little better with them—my family." She was convinced that her mother hated her, and she couldn't wait to move out: "If they only knew. I'm just counting time till I'm 18. Then they'll see."

During her last year of high school, Audre had a poem published in *Seventeen* magazine—her first taste of fame. She wanted to go to Sarah Lawrence College, in Yonkers, but it was too expensive. Disappointed, she decided she would apply to the more affordable Hunter College on Manhattan's Upper East Side.

That summer, during a Fourth of July trip to
Washington, DC, she and her family stopped at an ice
cream parlor. At this time the city's restaurants were
racially segregated, and the white waitress refused to
serve them. Audre was furious. She couldn't help
thinking that none of her friends from school would
ever have to experience this, and it added to her sense of
being an outsider: "a black girl in a society that was
basically white."

A few weeks later, during a fight with her sister
Helen and her mother, Audre announced that she was
moving out. She'd had enough. "My way must be always
forward from now on—I've burned all my bridges
behind me," she wrote in her journal. She moved into a
friend's apartment the very next day.

At Hunter College that fall, Audre studied English and philosophy. On Thursday nights, she took the train to attend meetings of the Harlem Writer's Guild, a group that had influenced many famous Black writers. Even within this group of writers, Audre felt like an outsider—in part, she said, because she was a lesbian.

She became involved with the gay community in Greenwich Village. She began publishing regularly and was active in civil rights, antiwar, and feminist movements. She spent a year as a student in Mexico, which she described as a time of great personal and artistic growth. When she returned to the United States she continued her studies to become a librarian, and then a professor of English. She helped start the first US publisher specifically for women of color— Kitchen Table: Women of Color Press. In 1991, she was named poet laureate for the state of New York.

Audre emphasized the importance of community in working for change and argued that we should see our differences as a source of strength rather than letting them divide us. She believed in the power of language to bridge differences, saying that "it is not difference which immobilizes us, but silence. And there are so many silences to be broken."

Audre wrote essays about racism and injustice, and she talked about the importance of speaking your truth:

"My silences had not protected me. Your silence will not protect you." She understood that speaking up could be difficult and scary, but argued that it is necessary to fight for the world we want. "When I dare to be powerful, to use my strength in the service of my vision, then it becomes less and less important whether I am afraid," she wrote. Later in her life, when she became ill, she wrote about her experiences with breast cancer, speaking out about a subject that she said was too often surrounded in silence.

Audre Lorde died in 1992, having inspired writers, artists, and activists around the world. Her work helped shape our understanding of racism, feminism, gender, and sexuality, and her words continue to have a powerful impact today.

Ai Weiwei

Something Else Is Possible

Ai Weiwei is a Chinese artist, architect, and activist. He uses his art—from poetry and sculpture to photography and film—to speak out about social and political issues and to work for change. But he spent his childhood years in exile, living in an underground dugout in the Gobi Desert.

Ai Weiwei's mother, Gao Ying, was a writer. His father, Ai Qing, was a university professor and one of the greatest modern Chinese poets.

Ai Weiwei was born on August 28, 1957, eight years after the People's Republic of China was founded under the Chinese Communist leader Mao Zedong. When Ai Weiwei was a baby, Mao's Communist Party was trying to hold on to power by getting rid of anyone who criticized the government. This was known as the Anti-Rightist Campaign. Because Ai Weiwei's father was very well known, the authorities decided to make an example of him and accused him of rightism. In fact, he had been a member of the Chinese Communist Party since the early 1940s, and earlier in his life he had been imprisoned because he was suspected of being a leftist!

The year Ai Weiwei was born, about thirty thousand people, many of them writers, teachers, and journalists, were accused of being rightists. Many of these people were sent to labor camps for what was called re-education. Among them was Ai Qing, now considered an "enemy of the people." Along with their parents, Ai Weiwei and his older stepsiblings, Lingling and Gao Jin, were exiled to a labor camp in China's far north, in a frozen and remote area in the Gobi Desert.

The family lived in an underground dugout, which had previously been used for farm animals. It had a leaky roof made from branches and mud, and Ai Weiwei and his brother shared a bed made from earth covered with stalks of wheat. "Living conditions were extremely harsh," Ai Weiwei recalled, "and education was almost non-existent."

Ai Weiwei's father was nearly sixty, but he was forced to do hard physical work, cleaning the community's toilets. "He never really had a chance to rest, even for one day," Ai Weiwei said. His father said that people never stopped using the toilets—so if he took a day off, there would be twice as much to clean up the next day! When Ai Weiwei was very young, he used to watch his father at work. "I was too small to help," he said. "He would make this public area very clean—extremely, precisely clean—then go to another one."

Seeing the way his father was treated was the saddest part of his childhood, he said. "It was terrible to see how my father had no way to defend himself and no one to complain to when other people bullied and insulted him." Ai Weiwei remembered his father coming home with his head black from ink that had been poured over him. The family endured constant hatred, discrimination, insults, and abuse designed to break his father's spirit.

Ai Weiwei's mother tried to find food for the family, but there was never enough to eat and Ai Weiwei's father went blind in one eye from being malnourished. The family gathered whatever they could find to eat, collecting sheep hooves that had been thrown away by butchers, and sometimes finding a piglet that had frozen to death. Ai Weiwei's mother was given the job of feeding the corn to the cows, and was reprimanded for stealing it to feed her own family.

As a child, Ai Weiwei knew no other life; everyone around him was living under the same difficult conditions. He was a sensitive child but liked making ice skates and experimenting with gunpowder. He also got involved in the complicated politics of the playground and could be very mischievous. His father nicknamed him Cao Cao, after an ancient Chinese statesman famous for his cunning.

In 1966, when Ai Weiwei was nine, China's Cultural Revolution began. Mao urged young people to protect Communist ideals by crushing any opposition. Schools shut down, and across the country, students formed paramilitary groups called the Red Guard. Wearing olive green army uniforms with red arm bands, these groups denounced and attacked anyone they saw as an enemy of the revolution—which often included their own teachers. Mao praised the students' actions and ordered the police not to interfere. The Cultural Revolution was a chaotic and violent decade, which did terrible damage to China's culture and claimed countless lives.

During this time, artists, writers, and intellectuals were seen as a threat. Ai Weiwei's father had a collection of books, including poetry and books about art and art history. The Red Guard used to come to their home in the camp and inspect the books, looking for anything that they didn't approve of. Finally, when Ai Weiwei was nearly ten years old, his father had to burn his entire collection. Ai Weiwei helped, burning the books page by page.

Ai Weiwei was never encouraged to read: "If I touched a book my father would say, 'Ah, put it down, it's not good for your eyes.'" Reading and writing were dangerous, he said: "The future was very clear in China—anybody with knowledge would be punished. You couldn't speak your mind because it could lead to death. So you wouldn't let somebody in your family read." But Ai Weiwei remembered his father teaching him about Roman history and talking about art and poetry.

Ai Weiwei learned important things from his mother too. "My mother was good-hearted, hardworking, and selfless. She was super clear on right and wrong," he said. One cold day when Ai Weiwei was young, he and his mother came across a woman and child who were begging. "Mother asked me to take off my padded jacket and hand it to the little boy, who was visibly shivering in the cold wind. I watched him as he put it on. When we got home, Mother steamed some mantou buns and brought them back out to the mother and son." He later said that this incident taught him that "human feelings could be shared and passed around," he said.

After ten years in exile, Ai Qing was sent to a new camp on the edge of the Gurbantünggüt Desert in northwestern China. His mother decided to go back to

Beijing and take Ai Weiwei's younger brother, Ai Dan, with her. Lingling went to live with her birth father and soon after, Gao Jin was sent away to school. Ai Weiwei and his father were alone in the harsh conditions of their new dugout home. To survive, Ai Weiwei learned new skills—like how to build a stove, make bricks, craft furniture, and deal with infestations of rats and lice. In the mornings, he attended classes along with a handful of other kids—and with help from his father's friends, he learned how to draw.

After a long fourteen months, Ai Weiwei's mother and Ai Dan returned—and Ai Weiwei realized how much he had missed them: "In our underground home there was now laughter and warmth and we were no longer lonesome and morose," he recalled.

In 1976, Mao Zedong died and the Cultural Revolution came to an end. Ai Weiwei was nineteen, and had spent his whole life in exile, but now he and his family were able to return to the city of Beijing. Ai Weiwei finished high school and enrolled in the Beijing Film Academy to study animation. He became one of the founders of a groundbreaking group of artists known as the Stars. Mao had said that art must serve the interests of the state, but the Stars were interested in the ideas of self-expression, democracy, and artistic freedom. As a young student, Ai Weiwei attended marches and rallies in support of democracy.

In 1981, Ai Weiwei moved to the US. He expanded his artistic practice beyond painting, taking up sculpture and photography. After more than a decade in Berkeley and New York, his father became ill and Ai

Weiwei returned to Beijing. There was little support for contemporary art in China, but he wanted to change that. He published books about the new generation of Chinese artists, founded a gallery, and held exhibitions. He built his own studio and made more sculptures and installations. Although he often provoked controversy— like the time he photographed himself breaking a very precious two-thousand-year-old vase—Ai Wewei became one of China's most famous architects and helped design the Bird's Nest stadium for Beijing's 2008 summer Olympic games.

Because he grew up in such difficult conditions, Ai Weiwei said that the happiest parts of his childhood were his fantasies. "When real life cramps a person, the imagination blossoms," he said. He imagined a world different from the one he lived in, a world "where pain and despair did not rule, where something else was possible."

As an adult, Ai Weiwei used art to try to create that better world, bringing attention to injustice and fighting for freedom. He started a blog, where he wrote about art and society. Then, in 2008, there was a devastating earthquake in Sichuan. Schools and other buildings collapsed and many lives were lost. At first, Ai Weiwei couldn't write about it at all. "People asked me why but, faced with such a tragedy, I was silenced," he said. But soon he began writing again, using his blog and his art to remember those killed by the earthquake and to criticize the government for its failures and human rights abuses.

Because of his art and his activism, Ai Weiwei's blog was shut down by the government and he was beaten by the police. In 2011 the authorities bulldozed his studio and put him in jail for his outspokenness. All around the world people protested his imprisonment, and after three months he was released. The following year, Ai Weiwei created a huge brick sculpture from the rubble of his destroyed studio.

After finally being allowed to leave China again in 2015, Ai Weiwei decided to go to Greece for a vacation. On the island of Lesbos, he saw boats filled with refugees coming ashore. This experience inspired him to use his new freedom to bring attention to the terrible suffering caused by the global refugee crisis. He traveled to twenty-three countries, visiting forty refugee camps, and produced the documentary film *Human Flow*. "I know what it feels like to be a refugee and to experience the dehumanization that comes with displacement from home and country," he said. "There are many borders to dismantle, but the most important are the ones within our own hearts and minds—these are the borders that are dividing humanity from itself."

Ai Weiwei's art is based in his strong concern for the value of human rights, his awareness of human suffering, and his belief that we are all connected to one another. "An artist must also be an activist," he says. "In this time of uncertainty, we need more tolerance, compassion and trust for each other since we all are one."

Shonda Rhimes

Shonda Rhimes is a prominent television writer and producer, and one of the most powerful people in Hollywood. She has won many awards for her work increasing diverse representation on television. As a small child, she was already creating dramatic stories starring the cans of vegetables in her mom's pantry!

Shonda was born on January 13, 1970, in the Chicago suburb of University Park. Her parents were both academics: her mother, Vera Cain, was a college professor, and her father, Ilee Rhimes Jr., was a university administrator. They met on a blind date and fell madly in love. Best friends and partners, they had many shared interests and were so close that they often finished each other's sentences. "I grew up with a front-row seat to what a happy, healthy marriage looks like," Shonda said.

Shonda was the youngest of their six children. The oldest was her sister Delorse, who was followed by Elnora, James, Tony, Sandie, and Shonda. Twelve years older, Delorse was an important role model for Shonda. She taught her younger siblings new dances, like the

Bump, and cornrowed Shonda's hair so tightly it made her head ache. Sandie was closest in age to Shonda; the girls were just two years apart, so they shared a bedroom and often played together.

As the baby of the family, Shonda was very much adored. Every time the kids argued over who would get the extra cookie, the argument would end with someone saying, "Give it to the baby." Shonda could always find someone to read her a story—or cheer her on as she made up stories. This was lucky, because making up stories was Shonda's favorite thing to do. Shonda was a born storyteller.

When she was small, Shonda's favorite place to spend time was the pantry. "My earliest memories are of sitting on the floor of the kitchen pantry . . . playing with a kingdom I created out of canned goods," she remembered. It was an unusual hobby for a three-year-old, but Shonda's parents embraced her quirkiness and creativity and let her play in the pantry for hours on end. In the kitchen, just outside the pantry door, Shonda's mom had a small black-and-white television, and the American news of the 1970s—particularly Richard Nixon and Watergate—made its way into the imaginary world Shonda was creating. "The big can of yams ruled over the peas and beans, while the tiny citizens of Tomato Paste Land planned a revolution," she recalled. "There were hearings and failed assassination attempts and resignations."

Even before she knew how to spell, she and her sister Sandie dictated stories into a tape recorder for their mom to type. Once she got a little older and outgrew the pantry, the library became her favorite place. She was much more comfortable with books than with other children. When her mom would shoo her outside to get some fresh air and sunshine, Shonda would grab a book and hide it down the back of her pants. Then she'd climb the willow tree in her backyard and read until she was allowed back inside.

Shonda liked reading more than playing, but sometimes Sandie would drag her away from her books. At night, the two of them would run around the backyard chasing fireflies and trying to catch them in glass jars so they could watch them glow. When it was time for bed, they would open their jars and release all the fireflies into the darkness.

Shonda often played pretend games with Sandie. Being older, Sandie usually took charge and led the way. She pretended to be Shonda's mother, and they played games like "Making Dinner" and "Mom Sewing." Sometimes their older sisters joined in too. When they played "Mom Shopping at the Department Store," Sandie and Shonda would lay out their doll clothes on a table, with little price tags on them, and then wait outside the room until one of their older sisters shouted that the store was now open. "That was our signal to hurry inside and be the first to get to the sale merchandise," Shonda recalled. The girls would pretend that a salesclerk was rude to Sandie, and then Sandie would stand up for herself so fiercely that the salesclerk would apologize and offer her a cheaper price. The game usually ended with Sandie demanding to speak to the pretend manager.

As she got older, Shonda wanted to make up her own games, not just follow Sandie's directions. She wasn't interested in pretending to shop or sew or make dinner. She wanted to use her imagination. Other kids might make their Ken doll marry their Barbie doll, but not Shonda. She made her Barbie pull Ken's head off and store her shoes inside it. Then she'd reattach Ken's head and make him drive her Barbie to the spy organization she secretly ran with Nancy Drew! That was much more exciting, Shonda thought.

Shonda's love of making up stories sometimes got her into trouble. When she was ten years old, she told the other kids at Saint Mary's Catholic School that her mom had escaped from Russia after trying to assassinate the country's president. Her teachers were not impressed, and Shonda spent recess in church, on her knees, reciting the rosary for the nuns.

Although she was very intelligent, school was not always a comfortable place for Shonda. She was sensitive and painfully shy, and she was often the only Black girl in her class. "I did not have friends," she recalled. While her parents embraced their daughter and loved the things that made her unique, her peers were not as accepting. "No one is meaner than a pack of human beings faced with someone who is different," she said. "I was very much alone."

Shonda began writing, filling one fabric-covered journal after another. "I created friends. I named them and I wrote every detail about them," she said. "I gave them stories and homes and families. I wrote about their parties and their dates and their friendships and their lives." These fictional characters felt very real to her. By escaping into her imagination, she found a way to create a safe place for herself during a time when her own life was difficult. Writing made her feel good. "Writing was who I was," she said. "Writing was ME."

As a teenager, Shonda went to Marian Catholic High School in Chicago Heights. She volunteered at a hospital, which led to an interest in hospital settings and may have helped inspire her hit TV show *Grey's Anatomy*. She got a job serving ice cream at Baskin-Robbins. And she took her first driver's education class—which was unexpectedly terrifying.

Shonda had studied the rules of the road, and she was excited to get behind the wheel. Her dad had promised that when she had her license, she could drive the family car to school. "Driving meant freedom," she said. But when she climbed into the driver's seat for her first lesson, she got a terrible shock: the instructor told her to start the car, drive down the road, and take the ramp on to the freeway! Shonda was petrified, but it didn't occur to her to say no. When they got back to the school at the end of the lesson, she burst into tears. "Did I hit anything?" she asked. The instructor turned pale; he had thought she was an experienced driver.

After high school, Shonda went to Dartmouth College, an Ivy League school in New Hampshire. She studied English and film, joined the Black Underground Theater Association, directed and performed in student productions, and wrote fiction. As a kid, she'd often felt invisible, alone, or left out. Now she wanted to tell stories that included everyone—and she wanted to share those stories with the world. Shonda was determined to create television shows that looked like the real world, with women, LGBTQ+ people, and people of color in important roles. She wanted everyone to see people like themselves on TV—and to learn about people different from themselves as well.

Best known as the creator, writer, and producer of the medical drama *Grey's Anatomy*, Shonda has been widely recognized for her work increasing diverse representation on television. She has won numerous awards, including a Golden Globe, been nominated for three Emmy awards, and been included in *Time* magazine's list of the one hundred most influential people—twice! The production company she founded is named Shondaland, after the fictional world she dreamed up as a child. "Shondaland, the imaginary land of Shonda, has existed since I was eleven years old," she said. "I built it in my mind as a place to hold my stories."

Elliot Page

> ## Like the Boys
> ## in the Movies

Elliot Page is an award-winning actor, producer, and director. He is also an activist who advocates for queer and transgender rights. He began his acting career as a kid, even though he lived 3,500 miles away from Hollywood!

Elliot was born on February 21, 1987, in Halifax—a small city in the Canadian maritime province of Nova Scotia. His father, Dennis Page, was a graphic designer, and his mother, Martha Philpotts, was a French teacher. Elliot was assigned female at birth, and given a girl's name—but he always felt like a boy. In 2020, when he came out as transgender, he chose the name Elliot for himself. It was the name of the main character in the movie *E.T.* "I loved *E.T.* when I was a kid and always wanted to look like the boys in the movies," he said. He even has a tattoo on his arm that says E.P. PHONE HOME.

Elliot's parents divorced when he was very young. As a child, he lived in two houses, spending two weeks of each month with his mother and two weeks with his father. Later he said that this may have given him the aptitude for being in new spaces all the time—a useful ability for an actor!

An athletic kid, Elliot was a talented soccer player and loved street hockey, snowboarding, and wrestling with his stepbrother. He also loved the outdoors; in Nova Scotia, he said, "You're just surrounded by so much beauty and stillness." Elliot could ride his bike to the woods to explore or jump in a nearby lake for a swim. He liked video games too and enjoyed playing them on his Sega Genesis—a game console that was very popular in the 1990s.

Although the people around him saw Elliot as a girl, that wasn't ever how he saw himself. "I knew I was a boy when I was a toddler," he said. When he played games, he always imagined himself as a boy. He wrote fake love letters and signed them Jason. At that time, McDonald's Happy Meals included two different kinds of toys: one for boys and one for girls. Elliot would always ask for the boy's toy. If he was given dolls instead, he cut their hair short. And he remembers how important it was to him to be allowed to cut his hair short, too; with short hair, other people were more likely to see him the way he saw himself. "I felt like a boy," he said. "I wanted to be a boy. I would ask my mom if I could be someday."

At a young age Elliot became interested in acting.

He joined the drama club at his elementary school—a
private school called Halifax Grammar School—and
began taking classes at Halifax's Neptune Theatre
School. In fifth grade, he performed on stage in a
production of *Charlie and the Chocolate Factory*. When
local actor John Dunsworth was looking for a talented
young performer for a new television show, Elliot's
drama coach mentioned that he had a talented student.
All the other kids had showed up for the first day of
rehearsals for *Charlie and the Chocolate Factory* clutching
their scripts, the coach told John. Except for Elliot: he'd
left his script at home, because he'd already committed
all his lines to memory.

John ended up casting Elliot in a television movie
based on the life of miners in early-twentieth-century

Cape Breton, Nova Scotia. It was called *Pit Pony*, and it was Elliot's first step into an acting career. "I sometimes think, what if I was sick that day the casting guy came into school?" Elliot said later. He wondered what his life would have looked like if he hadn't become an actor. Maybe he would have pursued his passion for sports and become a soccer player instead.

Pit Pony started out as a movie, but it also became a TV show that ran for two seasons. "When I started, I wasn't really conscious of what was going on," he recalled. "I just was happy to memorize lines and ride ponies."

One thing he wasn't very happy about was having to grow his hair long for the part in the TV show. For the movie, he had worn a wig. But as an actor, he had to look a certain way—and it didn't always fit with how he felt on the inside. This was a problem that would get worse the older Elliot became.

Elliot's mother had family in Toronto, and on one visit to the city they went to see *The Phantom of the Opera* together. Elliot learned the words to all the songs and asked his mom how he could learn to play the lead role. She told him that he'd need to go to university. "You'll come with me, right?" Elliot asked. His mom laughed. "Honey, by that time, I think you won't want me to," she said. She was an important influence on him, especially when it came to valuing education and wanting to do well in school. "My mom is so passionate about what she does that it made me respect teachers," Elliot said.

Elliot's success with *Pit Pony* led to more parts on TV shows and in movies, and he started to think about a career as an actor. By the time he was fifteen, he was playing more mature roles—roles, he said, "that required depth and passion." At sixteen, he moved to Toronto on his own to study at the Vaughan Road Academy's INTERACT program, which was designed for students who were heavily involved in acting, music, or athletics. The school allowed students to have flexible schedules so that they could take high school classes and pursue their careers at the same time.

That same year, he landed the lead role in a movie, which required him to travel to England, Germany, and Portugal—and he was finally able to cut his hair short again. This time, he decided to shave his head! Some of the teens at school teased him, but Elliot was more

comfortable. He was becoming very independent. As a young actor, he was supposed to be accompanied by an adult whenever he was on set. His parents were supportive, but they both worked full-time—and Elliot sometimes felt more relaxed on set without them there. Often, another adult on the set would be designated as his chaperone.

When Elliot returned to Halifax, he completed high school at the Shambhala School, which was based on Buddhist principles of mindfulness. He recalled, "They don't teach you Buddhism, but the way the school works stems from the philosophy. It's about openness." While there, Elliot said, he never felt like anyone was judging him. Instead, students could talk about and learn about whatever they wanted.

As a teenager, Elliot played soccer at a competitive level, but as his acting career took off, he realized he would have to give up the hours spent on the soccer field. Still, in between acting jobs, he was a regular teenager and tried to keep his life as normal as possible. His parents helped: "My parents just want me to remain balanced and healthy and stay the same grounded human being that I am," he explained. "They're incredibly supportive but they never push me . . . and I adore them for that. It's a perfect kind of a situation. We just trust each other."

Elliot began identifying as gay in high school, but he worried that being open about his relationships would hurt his career. He also started thinking more about gender. He disliked sexist stereotypes, and a lot of movies seemed to rely on them. He was interested in playing roles that shook up stereotypes instead of reinforcing them. He wrote a long essay for school in which he argued that it was absurd to divide people into two separate and distinct genders and assume that everyone is either a boy or a girl.

In 2007, at age twenty, Elliot's career reached new heights when he earned an Academy Award nomination for the movie *Juno*. He loved acting, but he didn't love all the attention it brought, or the relentless pressure to look a certain way. The constant compromises were taking a toll. By this time, he had told his parents that he was gay, but it would be another seven years before he came out publicly. On Valentine's Day in 2014, at a Human Rights Campaign conference focused on LGBTQ+ youth, Elliot gave a powerful and courageous speech. "I am here today because I am gay," he said. "Maybe I can make a difference, to help others have an easier and more hopeful time. . . . I am tired of hiding and I am tired of lying by omission. I suffered for years because I was scared to be out."

In 2020, he came out as transgender in a social media post. "Hi friends," he began, "I want to share

with you that I am trans, my pronouns are he/they and my name is Elliot." Elliot knew that being a well-known actor gave him a large platform. He also knew that lawmakers were pushing forward bills attacking the rights of transgender people, which would allow for discrimination against transgender people and limiting their access to health care. So he promised to use his platform to advocate for trans equality, and he began sharing his own story to raise awareness.

In 2021, Elliot was interviewed by Oprah and by *Time* magazine. He became the first transgender man to appear on the cover of *Time*, seven years after actress and activist Laverne Cox was featured by the magazine in an article describing transgender rights as "America's next civil rights frontier." Laverne Cox was the first transgender person to appear on a *Time* magazine cover. Like Elliot, she has used her platform to advocate for social justice and to urge people to listen to transgender people and to take the lead from them. It's a message that Elliot has echoed: "There's so much misinformation and lies," he said. "So please don't rely on news articles that frame this as a 'trans debate' or don't even include perspectives of trans people."

Elliot also uses social media to reach as many people as he can, in the hope that others will join him in supporting transgender and nonbinary people and protecting transgender youth by fighting against harmful laws, challenging misinformation, and working to end all forms of hate and discrimination.

Amanda Gorman shot to international fame when she delivered her stunning poem "The Hill We Climb" at the 2021 inauguration of President Joe Biden.

Born in Los Angeles in 1998, Amanda had a speech impediment as a child—which led her to become very good at reading and writing. She wrote her first poems in third grade.

A speech by activist Malala Yousafzai inspired Amanda to become a youth delegate for the United Nations, and at sixteen, she founded an organization to create writing and leadership programs for young people. A year later, she published her first book of poems, and in 2017 she was named as the first National Youth Poet Laureate.

Amanda has said she intends to run for president in 2036, but she is already making a difference in the world through her words. As she says, "Poetry and language are often at the heartbeat of movements for change."

Further Reading

Bibliography

There are many wonderful books about trailblazers and changemakers, including autobiographies (books written by the person about their own life) and biographies (books about noteworthy people written by someone else). This is a list of some of the main sources used by the author in researching and writing this book.

PART ONE

Kamala Harris

Harris, Kamala. *The Truths We Hold: An American Journey.* New York: Penguin Press, 2019.

Angela Merkel

Kornelius, Stefan. *Angela Merkel: The Chancellor and Her World.* London: Alma Books, 2014.

Radice, Mark, dir. *The Making of Merkel.* BBC Worldwide Ltd, 2013.

Stacey Abrams

Abrams, Stacey. *Lead from the Outside: How to Build Your Future and Make Real Change.* New York: Picador, 2019.

———. *Our Time Is Now: Power, Purpose, and the Fight for a Fair America.* New York: Henry Holt & Company, 2020.

Benazir Bhutto

Bhutto, Benazir. *Daughter of Destiny: An Autobiography*. New York: HarperCollins, 2007.

PART TWO

John Lewis

Lewis, John. *Walking with the Wind: A Memoir of the Movement*. With Michael D'Orso. New York: Simon & Schuster, 1999.

Lewis, John, and Andrew Aydin. *March: Book One*. Illustrated by Nate Powell. Marietta, GA: Top Shelf Productions, 2013.

Dorothy Pitman Hughes

Hughes, Dorothy Pitman. *Wake Up and Smell the Dollars! Whose Inner City Is This Anyway: One Woman's Struggle Against Sexism, Classism, Racism, Gentrification, and the Empowerment Zone*. Phoenix, AZ: Amber Books, 2000.

Lovett, Laura L. *With Her Fist Raised: Dorothy Pitman-Hughes and the Transformative Power of Black Community Activism*. Boston: Beacon Press, 2021.

Patrisse Cullors

Khan-Cullors, Patrisse, and Asha Bandele. *When They Call You a Terrorist: A Black Lives Matter Memoir*. New York: St. Martin's Press, 2018.

Marley Dias

Dias, Janice Johnson. *Parent like It Matters: How to Raise Joyful, Change-Making Girls*. New York: Ballantine Books, 2021.

Dias, Marley. "'Let Us Help You Lead': Marley Dias on Why Young People Must Be Included in the Fight for Racial Justice." *Elle*. July 21, 2020. https://www.elle.com/culture/career-politics /a33336406/marley-dias-black-lives-matter-essay.

———. *Marley Dias Gets it Done: And So Can You*. With Siobhan McGowan. New York: Scholastic, 2018.

PART THREE

Al Gore

Maraniss, David, and Ellen Nakashima. "Al Gore, Growing Up in Two Worlds." *Washington Post*, October 10, 1999. https://www .washingtonpost.com/wp-srv/politics/campaigns/wh2000 /stories/gore101099a.htm.

Turque, Bill. *Inventing Al Gore: A Biography*. Boston: Houghton Mifflin, 2000.

David Suzuki

Suzuki, David. *David Suzuki: The Autobiography*. Vancouver: Greystone, 2006

Greta Thunberg

Alter, Charlotte, Suyin Haynes, and Justine Worland. "Greta Thunberg, Person of the Year." *Time*. December 11, 2019. https://time.com/person-of-the-year-2019-greta-thunberg.

Thunberg, Greta, Malena Ernman, Beata Ernman, and Svante
Thunberg. *Our House Is on Fire: Scenes of a Family and a Planet in
Crisis.* New York: Penguin Books, 2020.

Mari Copeny

Copeny, Mari. "The Flint Water Crisis Began 5 Years Ago. This
11-Year-Old Activist Knows It's Still Not Over." *Elle.* April 24,
2019. https://www.elle.com/culture/career-politics/a27253797
/little-miss-flint-water-crisis-five-years.

"8-Year-Old Flint Girl Who Wrote Letter to Obama: 'I Wanted
Him to Know What Was Going On.'" *Time.* April 27, 2016.
https://time.com/4310492/8-year-old-flint-girl-letter-obama.

Lodi, Marie. "This 13-Year-Old Activist Is Making Meaningful
Change in Her Community and Beyond." *Romper.* May 25, 2021.
https://www.romper.com/parenting/this-13-year-old-activist-is
-making-meaningful-change-in-her-community-beyond.

Suggs, Ernie. "Mari Copeny: Activist, 11, Is Face, Voice of Flint
Water Crisis." *Atlanta Journal-Constitution*, Feb. 27, 2019.
https://www.ajc.com/lifestyles/mari-copeny-activist-face-voice
-flint-water-crisis/ltBhSYnuS7ViDK6W8DHeeP.

PART FOUR

Audre Lorde

De Veaux, Alexis. *Warrior Poet: A Biography of Audre Lorde.* New York:
W.W. Norton, 2006.

Ai Weiwei

Ai Weiwei. *Ai Weiwei Speaks.* With Hans Ulrich Obrist. London: Penguin Books, 2011.

———. *1000 Years of Joys and Sorrows: A Memoir.* Translated by Allan H. Barr. New York: Crown, 2021.

———, dir. *Human Flow.* 2017.

Shonda Rhimes

Rhimes, Shonda. *Year of Yes: How to Dance It Out, Stand in the Sun and Be Your Own Person.* New York: Simon and Schuster, 2015.

Elliot Page

McBee, Thomas Page. "Elliot Page Finally Feels 'Able to Just Exist.'" *Vanity Fair.* April 28, 2021. https://www.vanityfair.com/hollywood/2021/04/elliot-page-finally-feels-able-to-just-exist.

Steinmetz, Katy. "Elliot Page Is Ready for This Moment." *Time.* March 16, 2021. https://time.com/5947032/elliot-page-2.

Index

Hill, Donna, 102–3
Hughes, Dorothy Pitman, 66–76

I

immigration, 50–51, 165
India, 22–23, 44
integration, 45
Iron Curtain, 28
Islam, 20
Ispahani, Nusrat, 17, 18–19, 20, 25

J

Japanese internment camps, 121–25
Jentzsch, Herlind, 28–29

K

Kasner, Horst, 28, 29–30
Kasner, Margarethe, 30
King, Martin Luther Jr., 86, 88
Ku Klux Klan (KKK), 72

L

LaFon, Pauline, 131, 132, 133
Lee-Ridley, Melton (Ray), 67, 68–69
Lewis, Adolph, 81
Lewis, Eddie, 78, 82–83, 85
Lewis, John, 10, 77–90

Lewis, Willie Mae, 78, 79, 85
LGBTQ+ activists, 101–2, 174, 198–208
Little Miss Flint. *See* Copeny, Mari
Lorde, Audre, 164–75
Lorde, Frederick Byron, 165–66
Lorde, Helen, 165, 168, 170, 172
Lorde, Phyllis, 165, 168, 170, 172

M

Mao Zedong, 177, 184
March on Washington, 61–62, 88
Marshall, Thurgood, 50
Martin, Trayvon, 103
Merkel, Angela, 27–38
Merkel, Ulrich, 37
Montgomery bus boycott, 86–87

N

Nakamura, Setsu, 119–20
Nakate, Vanessa, 161
National Association for the Advancement of Colored People (NAACP), 72–73
Nawaz, Sir Shah, 17
Nevers, Scott, 106–7

O

Obama, Barack, 12, 154–56, 160

They're Little Kids with Big Dreams . . . and Big Problems!

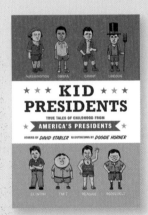

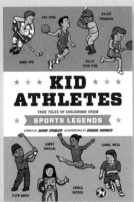

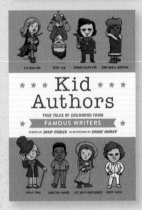

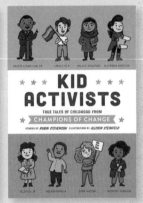

READ ALL THE BOOKS IN THE KID LEGENDS SERIES.

Available everywhere books are sold.

FOR MORE DETAILS, VISIT KIDLEGENDS.COM